SOWING THE SPRING

Sowing the Spring

Studies in British Poets from Hopkins to MacNeice

By James G. Southworth

Essay Index Reprint Series

BOOKS FOR LIBRARIES PRESS

FREEPORT, NEW YORK

First Published 1940

Reprinted 1968 by arrangement
with Basil Blackwell and Mott, Ltd.

INTERNATIONAL STANDARD BOOK NUMBER:
0-8369-0891-0

LIBRARY OF CONGRESS CATALOG CARD NUMBER:
68-54372

PRINTED IN THE UNITED STATES OF AMERICA
BY
NEW WORLD BOOK MANUFACTURING CO., INC.
HALLANDALE, FLORIDA 33009

To My Wife
(In Memoriam)
and
To My Father and Mother
this book is affectionately dedicated

Though winter's barricade delays,
Another season's in the air;
We'll sow the spring in our young days,
Found a Virginia everywhere.

TABLE OF CONTENTS

FOREWORD

THE absence of articles on Hardy and Housman from the present volume make it obvious that my purpose is not to attempt a comprehensive picture of modern British poetry. Although the essays have been written over a period of years (that on Binyon being much the earliest, but all of them before the outbreak of hostilities in 1939), the poets selected have not been chosen in a haphazard fashion. They show the impact of similar forces, chiefly political, on differently conditioned personalities.

My thanks are due to the editors of *The Sewanee Review* and *The Saturday Review of Literature* (New York) for permission to reprint the essays or parts of essays that have already appeared and to Mr F. W. Bateson who has helped see the volume through the press. My greatest indebtedness, however, must ever remain that to Dr A. J. Carlyle who as tutor and friend broadened far more than only my poetic horizon.

J.G.S.

Toledo, Ohio
September 1940

INTRODUCTION

MODERN poetry is our most accurate guide to contemporary life. It is accurate because, being poetry, it is not content only to impart current ideas, but through the medium of words carefully chosen for precision of meaning and sound with the technical aids of rhythm, rhyme, imagery, etc., it communicates the emotion aroused by those thoughts in minds possessing greater sensitivity and receptivity than are possessed by the average man.

Just as our knowledge of any problem is broadened by discussing that problem with all persons connected with it, so is our knowledge of modern life broadened by contacts with more than one poet. Our sympathies are challenged; and, if we are open-minded, enlarged. We must not expect poets more than other men to agree in their reactions which will be conditioned by their environment, education, and the age at which certain stimuli act upon them. Binyon, for example, with his roots firmly planted in the pre-war era, will differ as much from Eliot, as Eliot from younger men like Auden, Day Lewis, Spender, and MacNeice. He will also differ from Yeats and Lawrence because of the differences in their early environment. Hardy and Hopkins were writing at the same time, but their environment and education made different their reactions to life. Pervading all their work, however, is a time-spirit, present in varying degrees, that gives a uniqueness to their work that subtly sets it off from the work of an earlier age and makes it indigenous to its own period. The modern poet whose expression is not unique, who can use the idiom of an earlier age for the communication of his ideas, has little chance of survival even though he achieve popularity with his contemporaries; because a person who can utilize without alteration the idiom of an earlier day has not seen beneath the surface of his own age. He has sensed neither its rhythm nor those other qualities which give it its individuality. He can have little to say that is not obvious. Since the medium of his communication must reflect his own deepest convictions he can at best be only an anachronism.

To-day we attach little value to those poems of Tennyson that brought him widespread popularity, but we do cherish— as did such discriminating critics of his day as FitzGerald— those matchless lyrics of the 1842 volumes for which he incurred the charges of immorality and obscurity. Browning is no longer difficult; and no-one would now pronounce Wordsworth's 'Ode on the Intimations of Immortality' silly and nonsensical as did the contemporary reviewers. We should not be too hasty, therefore, in our denunciations of our contemporary poets. We must remember that genuine originality in anything is always at first hard to comprehend. Good poetry is no exception.

The person who approaches poetry unconditioned by an earlier exposure to the monuments of an earlier age has no greater difficulty with the modern than with the older poets; in fact, he frequently finds the moderns more readily comprehensible, because he is familiar with the experiences they are trying to communicate. Modern poetry does not aim at 'prettiness' because there is little prettiness in life for one who is courageous enough to view life squarely. In Auden, for example, the decaying and rotting aspects of nature have frequent place. Tumbled mine-heads against a desolate waste, like scenes in *The Waste Land*, image for Auden as for Eliot a decaying civilization. Since distance has been shortened by modern transportation, the poets are as familiar with the city as with the country. One finds, therefore, in their work the sordid and ugly aspects of city life in times of unemployment side by side with idyllic aspects of nature. The transitions being frequently sudden, the communication must impart that sharpness of contrast; the result is an expression that at first glance is difficult. But there is beauty, and in abundance; and even some sublimity. The conscientious reader of to-day's poetry is not an escapist. The escapist is the average man of the street who seeks comfort in detective stories, cheap romances, and in interminable movies of a sentimentalized life; one who is not willing squarely to face the issue of what is life's purpose, and what one is doing toward achieving it. The modern poet forces his reader into a realism so vivid that never afterwards can he view in the same light the world in which he lives.

The poets agree that evasion of life's problems is dangerous. Eliot sought to escape from the tortures of an offended idealism, but he has finally realized in *The Family Reunion* that escape is impossible. Whether a man be wealthy as the young host in Binyon's *The Supper* or whether he be a labourer in one of Lawrence's poems it is evident that spiritual death or nullity is the fate of the person afraid to confront life bravely. Lawrence and Yeats assure us that we cannot know where life will lead us —the goal is bound to be unknown, but we must be willing to accept the risks. We must learn from our experiences ever to reach higher; because unless we can profit from them we are but paltry beings. The full life necessitates a constant struggle against the *status quo*. Eliot's early poetry poignantly illustrating the despair that engulfs the person who, offended by the world about him, seeks to evade life, has given way to the later realization that the only result of evasion is a delayed maturity. MacNeice puts the case even more bluntly. Escapism, he says, is blasphemy. The poet cannot suffocate the great living beauty of the active life for the suffocating beauty of the ivory tower; and even if the struggle for life leads nowhere he must be willing to struggle. From the materials of life about him he must forge his own weapons for the struggle; from which 'blind collisions,' says Mr Day Lewis, man will come to know life thoroughly and, as a result, will finally understand the truth.

To be willing to struggle without the comforting illusions of what Robinson calls those 'fond old enormities' of heaven and hell requires courage. Without it, says Binyon, the world is dark; with it life becomes simple. Or, as MacDiarmid says, a man who has never faced death knows nothing of life. Courage, adds Lawrence, enables us to rid ourselves of such obstructions to life as self-importance, self-conceit, egoistic self-will, and helps us to cherish good, healthy natural feelings and instincts. As Mr Auden wrote first, and Mr Eliot later supported him, the comfort of any escape to an island of refuge from the problems of the world is but a temporary one. Even with the realization that men, taken as a whole, are pretty shoddy creatures content to be cabbages (making no attempt at a synthesis of their lives) rather than to be thinking organisms, that life is full of cruelty, hopelessness, indifference, and misunderstanding, that the search for beauty is along the wrong paths—even with this knowledge the poets in the present volume agree that there can be no relaxation in the search to put the greatest possible meaning into one's life. It may be that old age will bring the bitter realization (as it did to Yeats) that there is little one can actually know; but the person who has sought to know leaves far behind the person who would not exert the impulse to know.

The poets stress, too, the importance of courage not only as an aid in facing a restless world, but as a necessity in a restless world for independence of thought and action. Self-fulfilment is an adequate goal if looked at from a large enough point of view. Self-fulfilment, however, requires searching self-analysis and a close scrutiny of the validity of the existing code of taboos. A man must possess absolute integrity of thought and of action, and he must divest himself of those carelessly appropriated thoughts of others which his deeper consciousness is unable to accept. The great evil of contemporary life, as Lawrence constantly reiterates, is the tendency of man in a highly industrialized society to assume a cloak of humility and to make a sneaking evasion of his own consciousness. In a seemingly chaotic world like ours, insists MacDiarmid, we must find men who, rejecting what other men think, insist upon independence of thought. Like Lawrence, he has little use for the robot masses who have lost the spark of God and have let themselves become no better than the machines they tend. He realizes that their condition is due to their own mob cowardice, that they are not inherently noble, that even with every opportunity for a full life they would not know how to grasp it. They are not as equal to life as to the machines they tend. Auden and MacNeice are likewise fully alert to the inability of the masses to achieve rich lives for themselves. Without whitewashing the victims they all condemn the system which has brought about such a state. Spender overflows with pity for the victims of this industrialized society dominated by the robot classes. The case for self-fulfilment not possible in a heterosexual relationship is put by him and Auden. With great candor they have communicated their experiences. They have had the courage of their convictions and they have been willing to pay the price of being misunderstood. Unfortunately, however, they have been unable to rid themselves of a sense of guilt. Logically they know they are right, but something in their deeper self-consciousnesses prevents the perfect fulfilment they so ardently desire.

In spite of the inertia preventing the dissatisfied from making any attempts to alleviate their own dissatisfaction, in spite of the absence of Christian charity, the poets represented in the present volume have fought for their conception of justice. The younger men have discarded the loyalties to their own class in order to fight for the new order which will recognize man's inalienable rights.

Where many will feel that the modern poets fall down is in the solution they offer to the problem. Actually, they offer none. They recognize that thought and action are useless without vision and deplore its lack in present day society. The men in the fortunate positions of life have lost sight of reality. The financiers, scientists, educators, clergy, and politicians have not only lost their perspective but are apparently unaware of or indifferent to the growing restlessness among the workers. Spiritual barrenness is prevalent in every stratum of society. More than any other poet Mr Eliot has succeeded in communicating the intensity of this sense of barrenness to the readers. When reading his poetry we find ourselves in a state of willing suspension of disbelief great enough to obscure temporarily the one-sidedness of the picture. The poets are not only content, however, to point out the barrenness. They realize that once man is aware of the conditions, he must fight for a political system which will remedy them. He must take the long view. The practical solution is not the problem of the poet although several different solutions are suggested. The actual political system would make little difference as long as life itself would be given a chance. Democracy, said Lawrence, is service not to serve the common people, but is the service of the common people to life. Like Milton and Wordsworth, but with less power, the modern poets express their indignation at the abuses of our class society.

When the poets proselytize for specific remedies they fall down, and naturally so. They attempt to do something in poetry that properly belongs to the field of prose. Fortunately, however, there is little direct propaganda. All political opinions find utterance from the 'royalist' attitude of Eliot, through the liberal attitude of Binyon and Day Lewis, to the 'leftist' attitude most strongly represented by MacDiarmid, Auden, and Spender. Binyon, for example, believes it dangerous to blind oneself to the social unrest arising from the sharp cleavage between the 'haves' and 'have-nots.' The 'haves,' with nothing to gain and everything to lose, are content to do nothing. They seemingly lack the energy for action. The chief protagonist in Eliot's *The Family Reunion* finally realized this. The ordinary day of most of the people of his class was little more than breathing. Naturally they were bored with life and with one another. One can escape despair only through a life of activity.

Hopkins foreshadows the present attitude towards industrialized society. He was keenly aware of the slight benefits the industrialization of England and the expansion of empire brought to any but the ruling classes.[1] Lawrence had an even more intense hatred of the results of industrialization, a hatred arising from the fact that life has little chance, that it has made of man an automaton who has lost the power to assert his individuality, that he is no more than a cringing animal. Mr MacDiarmid, like Lawrence and Mr Eliot, is offended by the triviality of the life he sees everywhere about him. Recognizing that the old economic system is not the only valid one, he regrets that the 'have-nots' lack the will to bring about the finer life that could be theirs. If they but realized their power, they could alter conditions to benefit themselves. He is realist enough, however, to recognize that the masses by their body smells, their insensitivity, and their coarseness frequently offend those whose idealism impels them to help them. With all his pity for them Spender has frequently been repelled by their ordinariness. Auden, too, is keenly alive to the fact that the masses are themselves largely to blame for their condition. They lack sufficient vision to pursue their objectives beyond the point of satisfying their immediate needs. Mr MacNeice is aware of the sordidness of city life, particularly in the slums, and he knows that most of the 'have-nots' will not attempt to pull themselves out of their slough. Mr Spender, too, has witnessed the social conditions resulting from indolence and unemployment. Through his power to evoke pity for the unfortunates he arouses a vivid realization in the minds of his readers. Mr Eliot alone seems to have had little pity or understanding of the 'have-nots.' Their very presence offended him, although in justice to him it is not because they are 'have-nots.' It is because they lack spirituality. He castigates barrenness in whatever stratum he finds it.

Industrialization has not, however, been bad only for the 'have-nots.' Lawrence realized that the evil to the industrialists

---

[1]His friends accused him of 'red' tendencies.

as men was as great as that to the workers. Industrialization divided society between the robot-masses and the robot-classes on the one hand and the small remnant of the valuers of life on the other. The latter group is unfortunately rapidly being ground exceedingly small. MacDiarmid scorns those who toady to royalty just as he scorns royalty itself. He is vitriolic against the abuses of capitalism and regrets with Auden and the later Eliot that the would-be leaders fritter away their time, attaching undue importance to family. They are the victims of a wrongly emphasized education. It is clear that all the poets in the present volume have the same ideals, although each expresses his ideals in his individual way. They all have a powerfully developed social consciousness which aims at the betterment of the everyday life of all classes.

They are, of course, idealists; and their idealism persists in the face of realism. That is, they can take the world but as the world and yet believe that something finer will emerge. Some of the most powerful communication in Hopkins, Lawrence, and Eliot lies in the expression of the offence to their idealism. Hopkins, for example, keenly regretted the lack of self-discipline he saw everywhere about him. The complacency of the masses aroused Lawrence to a fury of indignation, just as for a time the barrenness of the world about him drove Eliot into himself. He has recently come to the realization that in spite of this all-suffocating, practically all-embracing barrenness man cannot give up the struggle for the spiritual things he so highly values. He now agrees with Binyon, Lawrence, and the younger poets that he cannot hold himself aloof. He must merge himself with the stream and attempt to change its course from within. The general strike of 1926, coming at an impressionable stage in the lives of young men whose idealism had as yet been unoffended, jolted Auden, Spender, Day Lewis, and MacNeice into an early realization of their problem. For the first time they saw at first hand the conditions which aroused the more intelligent labour leaders to attempt a remedy for oppressive conditions, and they wanted to be of assistance rather than to perpetuate the *status quo*. They have had to struggle to maintain their ideals in the face of discouragement arising from the indifference of those they would help and the active hostility of those who think they would lose by altering conditions. Mr Binyon, a liberal from the beginning, with his roots firmly planted in pre-war soil, was not disturbed by the upheaval of post-war years. The others are achieving a perspective that will enable them to work quietly and steadily towards their goal.

Discouragement has often come, but less frequently with greater maturity. Surmounting it, they have lost the fear of themselves. They have learned that to strive for the way they know to be the right way they must combat the reactionary forces of family, education, and religion. What is more important, increasing age no longer lets them anticipate an immediate Utopia. Only by constant effort over a long period will they to some degree be able to impinge their ideals on the world.

It is interesting to notice the unanimous denunciations of the traditional public school education by the younger poets. It would be the right education, they agree, were the *status quo* to remain unchanged, but it does not fit youth in a rapidly changing world; it keeps them in ignorance of the world in which they must soon take their place. To a great extent their charges are just, but no one has yet devised a general system of education that did not bring some hardship to the unusual child. When reading their vitriolic denunciation of the public schools one unconsciously thinks of the youthful Shelley of over a century and a quarter ago.

Bibliolaters are inclined to look upon the present age as an irreligious one. I am inclined to think, however, that rarely has there been a greater seeking after true religion than to-day. The poetry accurately reflects this search. Formalized religion, except to Eliot who turned to it in despair, has become the symbol of reaction. It is one of the most serious existing hindrances to the complete realization of the new order. The young poets—and they typify the problem of many people to-day—find in the church no expression of the Christian ethic which is spurring them to an enlarged social consciousness. The clergy are neither providing this rational faith, nor are they in their own lives setting an example that a person who looks upon religion as a truly spiritual thing is able or willing to follow. Because it would conserve all that it has gained, the church has not matured spiritually as rapidly as those who have unselfishly been willing to face danger. As a result the teachings of Christ are more heeded by the non-church-goers than by the goers. Thinking persons cannot follow the leadership of those who from fanaticism or for their belly's sake have crept into the fold. When they speak of the Christ-like ideal it is in a voice of hollow brass and tinkling cymbal.

Whether it be for one's fellow man—which has altered the direction of politics—or whether it be a personalized emotion, love is as important a motivation of poets as it has ever been. It is, says Binyon, one of the most potent means of uplifting the soul, which, according to Lawrence, is the deepest part of our own consciousness. It is that quality which enables man to achieve his greatest beauty, his greatest fulfilment. Whether it be love of man for humanity, for a parent, for a mistress, or, as in Auden and Spender, the love of man for another man, the value is the same. The frankness of treatment of the homo-sexual aspect of love makes more difficult the understanding of many poems by the latter two. They attempt to communicate to their readers an experience which many are unable to share in spite of the prevalence of the discussion of the subject. Either they cannot imagine it or the communication is flavoured by the intrusion of a mnemonic irrelevance. They will judge the poem from a moral rather than an aesthetic basis. Obviously, however, if one is to do justice to the emotion underlying many of Auden's and Spender's finest lyrics he must rid the term of any sense of morbidity. Not only love, however, but death, age, and mutability have inspired many beautiful lyrics. Lawrence is perhaps the most eloquent on death, and Yeats on mutability and age.

It will surprise many to know that patriotism is an important element in modern poetry. In fact, no poetry of any era strikes me as being so consciously patriotic as that of to-day, so concerned for the welfare of their country as are the younger poets. They detest the cheap, sentimental chauvinism that pays homage to political stagnation. Because a deep love for the country grips each poet in the present volume, except perhaps Eliot—MacDiarmid for Scotland, Yeats and MacNeice for Ireland, and the others for England—they would change conditions in order that she might be worthy of their love. The desire to remedy conditions under which great masses of the population live in a state of peonage and under which leaders as well as the masses are blind to the meaning of the abundant life cannot be branded as unpatriotic, even though many would call it so. Ameliorated conditions would make a rich heritage available to those whose need for the freshness and beauty of the countryside is great. The patriotic note at its best is like that of Burns for Scotland and of Milton and Wordsworth for England. The militant note of the latter two dominates modern poetry.

Nature poetry has a long and honourable heritage in English literature, a heritage to which the poets continue to pay homage. Of the poets in this volume Hopkins will undoubtedly take his place as a major nature poet. For sheer beauty of sensuous apprehension combined with an accuracy of observation that stirs one's admiration the more it is studied, Hopkins ranks high. Binyon and Day Lewis contain much of the spirit of Wordsworth: nature is a great regenerating force. It is not the unspoiled beauty of nature that attracts Auden; he prefers nature marred by the signs of industrial decay and he likes to view it from high places. Side by side, the beauty of the country and the stark ugliness of the city stand in sharp contrast, a

contrast heightened by MacNeice, Spender, Lawrence and
Eliot. Nature plays a relatively minor rôle only in the work of
Eliot who is essentially a town poet; and the few nature images
in his work are such as are visible in the city. The lack of the
alleviating power of nature accounts for much of his pessimism.

In their descriptions of the regenerating power of nature or
of her minutiae the poets have not combed the literary files for
their images. They have trained a steady eye on her and have
communicated their sharp reactions in correspondingly appro-
priate images. Binyon's images are 'easier' than those of the
other poets. Although typically Georgian, they are no less the
result of actual observation than are those of any of the others.
They are integral to the thought, not mere ornaments. With
Binyon and Lawrence no reader can experience difficulty in
understanding the images or ideas, except perhaps Lawrence's
conception of 'darkness.' With Hopkins the case is different.
The strict dialectical discipline of his training and his busy life
as a Jesuit combined to give a quality of bone and muscle to
his work that might not have been the case had he had more
leisure. His early work at least gives no hint of this later firm-
ness. His thinking is always clear and his images, even in the
description of Harry Ploughman, minutely accurate. Eliot is no
longer difficult except in a few isolated passages where his
phraseology carries an esoteric meaning. Auden remains difficult, but only in his early work when he indulges in private
jokes or when read in snatches. I confess, however, that I
never have made sense out of parts of *The Orators*. MacDiarmid
(if you can get past the barriers of his aureate terms), Day
Lewis, Spender, and MacNeice offer little trouble. None of
them, however, is as difficult as Shakespeare or Donne when
their minds are working at white heat at the expression of a
subtlety.

Anarchy does not apply to the poets in the present volume.
None is ignoring the tradition of poetry either in subject

matter or technique. They are, however, attempting to advance it in order that they may give adequate expression to
those things vital to them. They are merely experimenting in
putting their wine into 'steinies' and tins instead of into goat-
skins. Binyon and Lawrence are perhaps the least interesting
prosodically. They both are rich in the stuff of poetry, but
their expression possesses a laxity that robs that stuff of its
inevitability. Lawrence's courage in departing from what we
might call the Georgian tradition has been a powerful stimulus
towards independence for the younger poets. Greater has been
the influence of Hopkins who looked upon himself as strongly
traditional, traditional, that is, in the line of Shakespeare, Milton, and Dryden. There are qualities of Donne in him, too, but
he has made no mention of Donne in his writings. He was so
well versed in the tradition of poetry—he wrote and lectured
on poetry and rhetoric—that he was able to act with freedom.
Even his apparent innovations carried with them the authority
of Shakespeare and Milton. The vitality of his sonnets gave a
new impetus to this much-used-seldom-successful form that
has exerted a powerful influence on the younger school. Mr
Eliot, like Hopkins, has also worked in the tradition, at the
same time altering it, but with different masters for his models.
Of the younger group Mr MacNeice shows the greatest individuality in his prosodic experiments. He, too, is deeply
versed in classical tradition. But the diversity of influences has
been great. Conscious and unconscious echoes are constantly
heard of Spenser, Shakespeare, and the Elizabethans, of Donne,
Dryden, and Milton, of Shelley, Keats, Tennyson and Browning, Hardy, Whitman and Emily Dickinson—to name but the
most obvious. The new voices that have emerged are, however, decidedly modern.

One need not worry for fear poetry is disintegrating into
formlessness. As in Schönberg's latest string quartets the
apparent formlessness lies only in our ignorance. Study reveals
a form as definite as that in music or poetry of a more familiar

age. In spite of the many attempts that have been made at long poems, the genius of the age lies essentially in the lyrics. No modern long poem is an unqualified success, although many possess passages of great beauty.

Of the poets about whom I have written I make the claim of greatness for only two—Hopkins and Yeats. Of course it is still too early to know what the younger men might yet produce. Already one or two are showing signs of falling off. But as milestones in the history of English poetry all will be of use. Professor Radhakrishnan in his *Eastern Religion and Western Thought* summarizes the prevailing poetic attitude. He writes:

> To-day the soul of man no longer rests upon secure foundations. Everything round him is unsteady and contradictory. His soul has become more complicated, his spirit more bitter, and his outlook more bewildered. But his unrest is not a mere negative force. He is not only oppressed by new doubts but is inspired by new horizons, new perspectives, and a thirst for new relations with fellow men. He has reached a more advanced state of spiritual maturity, and so the dogmas of traditional religions are no longer able to answer his questions or overcome his doubts. The present profound *malaise* is really a form of growing-pains. The new world for which the old is in travail is still like an embryo. The components are all there; what is lacking is the integration, the completeness which is organic consciousness, the binding together of the different elements, making them breathe and come to life. We cannot live by instinct, habit, or emotion. We need a rational faith to sustain a new order of life and rescue us from our mental fag and spiritual anxiety.

GERARD MANLEY HOPKINS

'EVEN in Browning's best works,' wrote Gerard Manley Hopkins, in 1881, 'I always had an indefinable feeling that he was not thoroughly educated; i.e., that he had not taken poetry at the highest point at which it had been left by others, and so was, as it were, off the track.' The same charge will not be brought against Hopkins. He carefully examined the highest points to which Shakespeare and Milton had carried poetry, followed their example, and continued his prosodic experiments from a point at which theirs ended. Some of his innovations were accepted and used by the poets who were privileged to read his work during his lifetime, but Hopkins, knowing that he was right in what he did, was willing to wait for publication. 'I have no thought of publishing until all circumstances favour,' he once wrote, 'which I do not know if they ever will.' He refused to let an admirer publish one of the poems because 'if the paper takes the piece (which it is sure to misprint),' he wrote, 'few will read it and of those few fewer will scan it, much less understand or like it. (To be sure the scanning is plain enough, but people cannot, or they will not, take in anything however plain that departs from what they have been taught and brought up to expect: I know from experience).' The same attitude on the part of the reader is still active. I think the over-stress on his technical phraseology used for his prosodic innovations is one deterring factor, and a comparative silence on the part of his admirers about the subject matter of so concentrated a communication is another. But the effort to understand him pays large dividends. After a careful study of his work—and he is unquestionably one of our most passionate poets—no one can ever again view in the same way the vast corpus of mid- and late-Victorian poetry. He is of his age, but he dwelt apart.

Since 1918, the date of first publication of his poems, his influence has widened until one can truly say that he has exerted a powerful influence in straightening the course of the tradition of English poetry. I think the time will come when the publication of the *Poems of Gerard Manley Hopkins* will be looked upon as an important landmark; as important, probably, as the publication of Spenser's *The Shepherd's Calendar*, Percy's *Reliques*, and Wordsworth's *Lyrical Ballads*. No young English poet of significance is free of his influence. One of the latest but most important arrivals on the poetical scene, Mr Louis Mac-Neice, shows the greatest influence of all. Nor is it due to chance alone, Hopkins was and MacNeice is deeply steeped in the classics.

To many readers, however, he remains an unread poet. In America, for example, few professor-editors of anthologies for the so-called 'survey' courses include selections from his work, although they continue to include copious selections from poets who, one now realizes, were of their time, and only that. Nor does he receive mention in a book on the reading of poetry that has but recently come to my desk.

One need not regret that Hopkins' busy life afforded him but little time for poetry. I think his work is the richer for it. In that he resembles Gray. His poems underwent a long germinating process evident in the result. 'I cannot in conscience spend time on poetry,' he wrote in 1879, 'neither have I the inducements and inspirations that make others compose. Feeling, love in particular, is the great moving power and spring of verse and the only person that I am in love with seldom, especially now, stirs my heart sensibly and when he does I cannot always "make capital" of it, it would be sacrilege to do so. Then again I have myself made verse so laborious.' But it was not only time that was lacking, it was sustained inspiration. Writing in 1888, he said: 'It is now years that I have had no inspiration of longer jet than makes a sonnet, except only in that fortnight in Wales: it is what, far more than direct want of time, I find most against poetry and production in the life I lead.'

Hopkins nowhere more effectively reveals his poetic powers than in his sonnets. Of the fifty-one finished pieces, thirty-four are achievements in this difficult genre and are of a sufficiently high quality to assure him a place as one of the great sonneteers in English poetry. His sonnets are not merely fourteen line poems like the general run of so-called sonnets. They are carefully wrought entities following a definite structural pattern. He laid down certain rules for sonnets in his letters to Canon Dixon, and unlike that of many poets his practice conforms to his theory. I do not wish to enter into a detailed discussion of his theory, but a summary of the main points will be useful. The Italian sonnet was, he thought, the only true form. The octave should be strictly marked off from the sestet and a corresponding maintenance of the proportions within the octave (two quatrains) and the sestet (two tercets) upheld. In other words, in order to get the greatest beauty from the sonnet the lines should be grouped $4+4+3+3$. Such a division gives symmetry in the octave and sestet but makes the two major divisions unsymmetrical. The discussion of the subject matter will illustrate this practice of division. Since the English sonnet is notably shorter than the Italian, resulting from the heroic line of the latter being longer than that of the former and from the greater length of the syllables in the latter language, English poets if they would avoid a lighter, more tripping, and more trivial quality than that possessed by the Italian must compensate for this difference by various devices. The simpler of these are gravity of thought and greater weight on the syllables themselves. He preferred mechanical remedies— either the introduction of 'outriding' feet[1] or the use of Alexandrines.[2] 'Henry Purcell' and 'Felix Randall' are examples of his practice in lengthening by six-stress lines, the extreme ex-

[1]'An outriding foot is, by sort of contradiction, a recognized extra-metrical effect; it is and it is not a part of metre; not part of it, not being counted, but part of it by producing a calculated effect which tells in the general success.' *Letters of G.M.H. to R.B.* (1935), p. 45.

[2]Hopkins' Alexandrines are lines of six stresses, not necessarily the regular twelve-syllabled lines of English poetry.

ample of which is 'Spelt from Sibyl's Leaves'—the 'longest,'
said Hopkins, 'ever made; longest by its own proper length of
its lines.' 'Tom's Garland,' 'Harry Ploughman,' and the Hera-
clitean Fire sonnet are longer by the use of codas. I do not
think 'Felix Randall' and 'Spelt from Sibyl's Leaves' as successful, however, as most of the other thirty-one. He tried to com-
press too much thought within the bounds of a sonnet, even in
those in which he used codas. I once thought 'Harry Ploughman' a case in point, but with each reading it becomes richer in
meaning. In his desire to make Harry Ploughman stand out as
a vivid figure within fixed prosodic limits he was compelled to
wrench the syntax to fit his needs. He himself felt that 'dividing
a compound word by a clause sandwiched into it was a desperate deed,' and did not think the result an unquestionable success. It takes a Hopkins enthusiast to face the problem. The
thrill of decoding is exhilarating: and a generation trained on
some of our younger poets will find the solution much simpler
than do those of an older generation.

But what is the thought underlying the poems? What subjects interested him? The simple answer would be to say they
are all essentially religious in theme, arising from his deep absorption in his profession of Jesuit. Since he was a convert to
Catholicism he undoubtedly took his religion more seriously
than one born in the church and was probably a frequent trial
to his brothers. We must remember, too, the great influence
exerted by Cardinal Newman on the Oxford youth of the
1860's. But, except for a few poems written to commemorate a
particular occasion, I do not think that their inspiration was
primarily from this source. The resolution of the theme might
be religious, but not the theme itself. Religion was the impulse
that gave greater universality to what would otherwise be only
a beautiful descriptive poem. His notebooks, journals, letters,
and drawings reveal an intense absorption in beauty and its
various manifestations. He is particularly struck by the minutiae as well as by the larger aspects of nature. Physical beauty

also possessed a great attraction for him, but he felt that to be dangerous;[1] a greater attraction was beauty of mind, and greatest of all, beauty of character. His poetry reflects in a concentrated and concrete form these same interests. His prose works, in other words, document but do not add to his poetry.

The notebooks and journals, to be more specific, are filled with minute observations of changing cloud formations, the foam on waves, light, trees and their foliage, fish markings, and birds' songs. This interest overflows into his letters in comment that attests the accuracy of his ear and eye. He wrote to Bridges, for example, about the song of the cuckoo: 'I have been studying the cuckoo's song. I find it to vary much. In the first place cuckoos do not always sing (or the same cuckoo does not always sing) at the same pitch or in the same key; there are, so to say, alto cuckoos and tenor cuckoos. In particular they sing lower in flying and the interval is then also least, it being an effort to them to strike the higher note, which is therefore more variable than the other. When they perch they sing wrong at first, I mean they correct their first try, raising the upper note. The interval varies as much as from less than a minor third to nearly as much as a common fourth and this last is the time when the bird is in loud and good song.'

He looked upon the poets of the Lake school as faithful but not rich observers of nature; but Keats, a member of the school of Shakespeare and the Elizabethans, was a great realist and observer of nature. Hopkins' own poetry places him in this school. The few remaining exercises antedating his entrance into the Society of Jesus, when for seven years he ceased writing poetry, are obviously modelled on Keats, Shakespeare, and Milton. In his best work the sensuousness of Keats and the rhythms of Shakespeare and Milton with perhaps, as he admitted, a slight echo from Whitman combine to form a new

---

[1]The minutely accurate description of Harry Ploughman written *con amore* reveals the greatness of the attraction. One is reminded of some of Michelangelo's figures.

voice.[1] He stands in the first rank of nature poets. His accurate observations, not always obvious at first glance, are concentrated into the narrowest possible limits. Rarely, however, is nature the sole subject. It is of relatively minor importance in 'The Wreck of the Deutschland,' but it dominates at least ten of his thirty-one completed sonnets. Frequently, indeed, the octave is wholly given over to nature description leaving the 'argument' for the sestet.

After analysing one of his richly-detailed, highly-condensed, carefully-patterned nature poems one is not surprised to read in his letters that verse composition was a 'slow and laborious' thing.[2] It requires intense alertness on the part of the reader if he is to capture the sensuous beauty that floods his verse. In 'Starlight Night,' for example, the first quatrain describes the stars and starlight, the second, the transforming effect on the earth. Not only is the music of 'wind-beat whitebeam' effective, but the picture is accurate and definite. The wind revealing the under side of the leaves of the whitebeam—whitish in colour, therefore showing up in the starlight—and forming the 'airy abeles' (the poplars) into shapes like restricted flame from a flare, and his use of 'flake' to describe doves in such a light—'Flake-doves sent floating forth at farmyard scare!'—are magically fused.

There is joyousness as well as lushness (which, however, is out of keeping with the Virgin Mary) in the description of spring in 'The May Magnificat':

> When drop-of-blood-and-foam-dapple
> Bloom lights the orchard apple
> And thicket and thorp are merry
> With silver-surfed cherry

[1] 'But first I may as well say what I should not otherwise have said, that I always knew in my heart Walt Whitman's mind to be more like my own than any other man's living. As he is a very great scoundrel this is not a pleasant confession and this also makes me the more desirous to read him and the more determined that I will not.' *Letters to Robert Bridges* (1935) p. 155 (Oct. 18. 1882).
[2] One must not overlook the importance of the Jesuitical training in dialectic as an influence in his logical pruning of all excrescences from his verse.

And azuring-over greybell makes
Wood banks and brakes wash wet like lakes
And magic cuckoo call
Caps, clears, and clinches all—

Housman speaks of the cherries in blossom as being hung with snow along the bough. How much richer is 'silver-surfed,'[1] especially in conjunction with 'drop-of-blood-and-foam-dapple' as an epithet for 'bloom' and 'azuring-over' for 'grey-bell.'

The octave of 'Spring' is pure sensuousness. The opening itself justifies Hopkins' theories of stress. It begins with a positive statement that admits of no qualification, then proceeds with a convincing, accurately-described enumeration of the things that make spring so beautiful:

Nothing is so beautiful as spring—
When weeds in wheels, shoot long and lovely and lush;
Thrush's eggs look little low heavens, and thrush
Through the echoing timber does so rinse and wring
The ear, it strikes like lightnings to hear him sing;
The glassy peartree leaves and blooms, they brush
The descending blue; that blue is all in a rush
With richness; the racing lambs too have fair their fling.

The pounding of the sea on the rocks in the first quatrain of 'The Sea and the Skylark'; that of the lark's song in the second; the flight of the falcon in 'The Windhover'; the autumn scene in 'Hurrahing in Harvest'[2] ('the outcome of half an hour of extreme enthusiasm as I walked home alone one day from fishing in the Elwy'); the catalogue of 'dappled things' in 'Pied Beauty'; and the very different picture of the black boughs against a dark sky in 'Spelt from Sibyl's Leaves'—

Only the beak-leaved boughs dragonish damask the tool-smooth bleak light; black,
Ever so black on it——

[1] One of his drawings is an attempt to catch the quality and pattern of surf.
[2] The reader should compare this with Keat's 'Ode to Autumn.'

are but a slight indication of his power in evoking a picture in which the reader shares the poet's vivid experience.

The burden of the poems in which nature plays an important part has, however, a wider application. It is not only that all this beauty is from God, but that man is so care-bound he is unaware of this beauty about him. Absorbed in the business of getting and spending he takes no thought of the present nor of the hereafter, as a result of which the world has a care-worn brow. 'God's Grandeur' imparts the same concern over man's absorption in mundane problems—

> And all is seared with trade; bleared, smeared with toil;
> And wears man's smudge and share's man's smell: the soil
> Is base now, nor can foot feel, being shod;

just as in 'The Sea and the Skylark' he asks why man—'life's pride and cared-for crown . . . drains fast towards man's first slime.' 'In the Valley of the Elwy' he castigates the Welsh as not equal to the beauties of the country. Nature's beauty is always with us, but men rarely see it ('Hurrahing in Harvest'). Only on the one occasion I have already cited does Hopkins revel in a sensuous description of spring that ill accords with the basic idea of the poem.

Not only does the poet regret that man is so rarely conscious of the beauty of the natural world about him, but he regrets what man has made of man and of himself. He saw enough instances of promising youth develop into disappointing manhood to realize that only by a continuous devotion to the service of God through the periods of youth, prime, and age could one achieve a mature mind. It is necessary to insist, I think, that when Hopkins stresses 'service to God' he employs the expression in a broad sense rather than a narrowly protestant theological one. Such at least I think he means in 'Morning, Midday and Evening Sacrifice' in which the three ages of man are compared to three periods of the day.

He is moved by youthful innocence and purity ('The

Bugler's First Communion' and 'The Handsome Heart'), and he regrets that men have seemingly fallen away from Christ. His age was to him an ungodly one, a natural feeling to one of his purity. He regretted the lack of self-discipline he everywhere saw about him and stressed the fact that man is always at his best under a self-imposed discipline, not under one forced upon him. He was an intense idealist in a world which outraged his ideals. The positive side of the picture is 'The Brothers' which reveals a spiritualized homo-sexuality, an emotion evident in many of his letters to Bridges. 'Felix Randall,' 'Tom's Garland,' and 'Harry Ploughman' exemplify what in an early letter he termed his 'red' tendencies, tendencies enhanced by his work in the industrial centres. In a day when few poets were concerned with the problem of the common man, Hopkins constantly saw about him how little benefit the industrialization of England and the expansion of empire were to any except the ruling classes. His social consciousness was as advanced as his prosodic experiments.

His interest in his fellow men is further explained in the beautiful epithalamion for his brother's wedding, 'At a Wedding March,' 'The Candle Indoors,' and 'The Lantern out of Doors.' He throws further light on his interests in 'Duns Scotus's Oxford,' 'Henry Purcell,' and 'The Leaden Echo and the Golden Echo.'

One group of sonnets merits special attention—those dealing with the state of 'spiritual dryness' which brought him much suffering. It is evident in 'The Wreck of the Deutschland' that he sometimes experienced that feeling common, I believe, at some time or other to all persons in orders. It is the theme, however, of the sonnets 'My own heart let me more have pity on' and 'Thou art indeed just, Lord,' and appears in several others of the later period when he was worn out with over-work and ill health. These possess a directness, a passionate fire, and an autobiographical value that give them great importance in his work. Many letters to Dixon and Bridges support their thought; one passage in particular gives a clue: 'All impulse fails me,' he wrote to Bridges on January 12, 1888, 'I can give myself no sufficient reason for going on. Nothing comes: I am a eunuch—but it is for the kingdom of heaven's sake.' It might have been 'for the kingdom of heaven's sake,' but it also resulted from the constant assaults made on his intense idealism. He could not take the world but as the world, and it would not and could not live up to his ideals.

II

Hopkins' importance in English poetry does not, however, lie entirely in what he says, although he says it with passion. He is one of our most important innovators in prosodic form. His innovations, however, as with all important ones have tradition behind them. But before considering the problem of form, let us examine an aspect of his poetry that both helps to determine and is determined by that form—his imagery. This is an obstacle for many readers, but a surmountable one. I have already touched on the problem in a discussion of his subject matter. He packs his verse with a wealth of concentrated and unfamiliar, though accurate, images good enough to bewilder the person making his first approach. But so do Shakespeare and Milton; and so does every original poet.

Hopkins' poetry is difficult, but, as I have already suggested, he more than repays the effort. His thinking is never vague nor are his images ever muddled, although the omission of relative pronouns (e.g. 'Squander the hell-rooks [that] sally to molest him'), a frequent change of order (e.g. 'own my heart' for 'my own heart'), and his tendency to use to its limits that characteristic of English that permits a word commonly associated with one part of speech to do the work of another (as a noun acting as verb, etc.,) add to the difficulty of comprehension. On the whole, however, he is careful to avoid inversions because he felt they weakened or destroyed 'the earnestness or in-earnestness of the utterance.' He also eschewed such time-worn words as *ere*, *o'er*, *wellnigh*, *what time*, *say not* (for *do not say*) because, although dignified, they neither belonged to 'nor ever could arise from, or be the elevation of ordinary modern speech.'

In first-rate poetry the images serve a dual purpose. They form an inseparable part of the poem's structural design and they intensify the poet's communication. Design was important to him, so important, in fact, that he was willing to risk for it the charge of oddness. 'But as air, melody, is what strikes me most of all in music,' he wrote to Bridges, in 1870, 'and design in painting, so design, pattern or what I am in the habit of calling "inscape" is what I above all aim at in poetry. Now it is the virtue of design, pattern, or inscape to be distinctive and it is the vice of distinctiveness to become queer. This vice I cannot have escaped.' To achieve greater accuracy he makes extensive use of compound epithets. Passages already cited illustrate this characteristic and no poem is without its full quota. They strike the inattentive reader as meaningless and many an attentive reader as forced. Familiarity to a great extent dispels the latter reaction. 'Dare-gale' gives a far different impression of the skylark than does Shelley's 'blithe spirit,' although both are correct. But it indicates the strength and imagination which the poet injects into his epithets. He heightens the burdenlessness of a self-imposed discipline by the implied comparison of a rainbow on the meadow—'meadow-down is not distressed for a rainbow footing it.' It is pure music. The omnipresent and ubiquitous quality of God is admirably caught in his comparison of His grandeur flaming out 'like shining from shook foil.' He had in mind gold foil or gold leaf. Single words, too, like 'bleared,' 'smeared,' and 'seared' have a concreteness that makes the image unmistakable.

One of his most effective images occurs in 'The Wreck of the Deutschland' when he compares himself to the running sand in an hourglass:

> I am soft sift
> In an hourglass—at the wall
> Fast, but mined with a motion, a drift,
> And it crowds and it combs to the fall:

Time after time as a child I have reversed the hourglass particularly to watch the sand crowd and comb to its fall. The balance of the stanza telling us how through discipline he steadied himself transfers our attention to the lower part of the glass:

> I steady as a water in a well, to a poise, to a pane,
> But roped with, always, all the waydown from the tall
> Fells or flanks of the voel, a vein
> Of the gospel proffer, a pressure, a principle, Christ's gift.

The image bolsters the design of the poem by the manner in which he places the last word of the image at the beginning of a line for the purpose of stress. The position of 'fast' in the foregoing metaphor of the hourglass is but one example of a frequently used device. He gives greater force to the grandeur of God, when he builds up to 'crushed' at the beginning of the fourth line:

> The world is charged with the grandeur of God.
> It will flame out, like shining from shook foil;
> It gathers to a greatness, like the ooze of oil,
> Crushed. Why do men then now not reck his rod?

Just as the position of 'mounts' in 'Andromeda' intensifies the upward sweep:

> All her patience, morselled into pangs,
> Mounts.

Even more striking is the emphasis he gives to 'back' (which he thought an ugly word) by placing it in a stressed position at the beginning of the second line in 'The Leaden Echo.' His deliberate striving for this effect is apparent in the opening of 'Spring and Fall'—

> Margarét, áre you grieving
> Over Góldengrove unléaving?

He rejected 'concérning Góldengróve' because when the measure had four feet he was careful if one line had a heavy ending (e.g. 'grieving') to begin the run-over next line with an initial stress (e.g. 'óver').

One frequently loses sight of the image because of the metrical effects in which it is imbedded. Delight in the sheer musical beauty in 'Góldengrove unléaving,' for example, is apt to obscure the accuracy of the autumn picture condensed into two words. This is unfortunate, but it happens only to the inattentive reader. I cannot sufficiently stress the importance of approaching Hopkins with all the senses alert. One must be prepared to find in the same line combinations of three types of rhyme: i.e. alliteration (initial half-rhyme), assonance (single or double vowel rhyme: meet-sleep; meeting-evil), and 'shothending' (final half-rhyme: find-band; sin-run). Unlike Swinburne (of whom Hopkins said that everything he wrote was 'rigmarole,' that his words were 'only words,' and that his anapaests and dactyls were halting to his ear, and that his poetry lacked feeling and character) Hopkins' use of these devices fortifies, rather than obscures his meaning. In one line in 'The Wreck of the Deutschland' he epitomises the terror of the tragedy:

> And frightful a nightfall folded rueful a day
> Nor rescue . . .

or,

> Night roared, with the heart-break hearing a heart-broke rabble.

The unexpected cry of the nun to Christ to come quickly brings a sudden change in the poem:

> Why tears? is it? tears; such a melting, a madrigal start!

'Madrigal' is the right epithet, just as is 'reaving' (to indicate 'robbing,' 'plundering,' 'carrying off') in the latter part of the poem. The same technique with a different purpose is used in 'Peace' in which he asks Peace, a wild wooddove, when she will cease roaming around him and nestle under high boughs with her shy wings shut. Alliteration, consonant chiming ('. . . I got in part from the Welsh, which is very rich in sound and imagery'), repetition, assonance, internal rhymes, and subtle vowel gradation combine to heighten the effect of the image:

> That piecemeal peace is poor peace. What pure peace allows
> Alarms of wars, the daunting wars, the death of it?

He achieves a haunting musical effect together with a delicate and accurate image in the first stanza of 'Binsey Poplars'; particularly important is the position of 'shadow,' placed to receive the same stress it would carry in prose:

> My aspens dear, whose airy cages quelled,
> Quelled or quenched in leaves the leaping sun,
> All felled, felled, are all felled;
>> Or a fresh and following folded rank
>> Not spared, not one
>> That dandalled a sandalled
>> Shadow that swam or sank
> On meadow and river and wind-wandering weed-winding
> bank.

He also pairs words of different syllabic length yet similar enough so that the change in stress creates a subtle musical effect as in 'wildness-wilderness' ('Inversnaid') and 'disremembering-dísmémbering' ('Spelt from Sibyl's Leaves').[1] One could multiply indefinitely examples of his prosodic achievement and still do little more than scratch the surface. I still feel

---

[1]Hopkins was keenly alert to the value of vowel sounds. He recognized, for example, that the short-i sound in 'bidst' is longer than in 'bids', and in 'bids' longer than in 'bid', which in turn is longer than in 'bit'. He admired Milton's acute ear in making use of his consonantal endings.

that I have done no more than scratch the surface of even one of his good sonnets. Since beginning this essay I have constantly had to revise my opinion of certain poems; it has been a steady revision upward.

III

It would be a useless task to attempt here a study of Hopkins' influences. His letters tell us all we need to know. They reveal the qualities he admired in Shakespeare, Milton, Dryden, Keats, Wordsworth, and others in the vast panorama of English literature and what prosodic achievements he admired in the Greek and Latin poets. And although he mentioned that the more carefully he studied and admired the work of a man the more individual he tried to make his own, a subconscious influence was, nonetheless, undoubtedly present. Hopkins in turn is powerfully affecting the poetry being written today. His influence will be both good and bad. At his best his rhythms are strong, masculine, and of his time. In an age of diffuseness he sought to make his lines of thought compact; at a time when utterance was overwhelmed with fake medievalism, he exercised great care to make his diction strictly contemporary; when freshness of image was giving way to shopworn formulas he loaded his verse with an infinite wealth of observation. He wrote but little, but of how many poets can it be said that there is so little dross as in his? Unfortunately, too many young poets uneducated in the tradition of English poetry and anxious to be original will seize on Hopkins' oddities, expand them *ad nauseam*, and pervert the basic poetic tradition. But their work will soon find itself in the limbo of fools, and its influence forgotten.

It is not necessary to understand 'logaoedic' and 'sprung' rhythms, 'outrides,' 'over-rove,' etc., in order to catch the subtle music that pervades his verse; but it is necessary to read with all faculties alert, to pay strict attention to the meaning just as it is necessary if one is to interpret music to study care-fully the composition. Sight-reading of either never reveals but the most obvious beauties. Only by study can one measure its significance, grasp its infinite subtlety, its delicacy of nuance.

Hopkins shared with Wordsworth the strong conviction that the poetical language of an age 'should be the current language heightened, to any degree heightened and unlike an obsolete one.' He meant a normal heightening and excluded 'passing freaks and graces.' Or, as he elsewhere expressed it, 'a perfect style must be of its age.' He believed, and time has justified him, that the failure to meet this test would 'be fatal to Tennyson's *Idylls* and plays, to Swinburne, and perhaps to Morris.'

He strove for and succeeded in finding a rhythm for poetry (as Shakespeare and Milton did)[1] which he felt to be nearest the rhythm of prose, one that was 'the native and natural rhythm of speech, the least forced, the most rhetorical and emphatic of all possible rhythms'; one that combined opposite and (as he said one would have thought) incompatible excel-lences—'markedness of rhythm . . . and naturalness of expres-sion.' To see the close affinity between his prose and poetry one need only refer to his *Journals*, obviously by the same hand as the poetry; better still, he need only read the opening line of each sonnet. They are strikingly Donne-like in their directness. They differ little from forceful prose.

Since English verse is accentual (and to be spoken)[2] a stressed syllable may be equal to one or more weak syllables. A metrical foot consists in Hopkins' prosody, therefore, of

---

[1] In his letters Hopkins lists several examples:

Whỹ should this desert be?	(*As You Like It*)
Thóu for whóm Jove would swear	(*Love's Labour's Lost*)
Hóme to his Móther's hóuse prívate retúrned	(*Paradise Regained*)
Thís, this is hé, sóftly a whíle	(*Samson Agonistes*)

[2] 'Quantitative verse, as in Greek or Latin is sung or chanted, accented verse, as ours, is spoken. French verse is counted. Italian is spoken and counted too.' *Notebooks of Gerard M. Hopkins* (1937), p. 237.

from one to four syllables only one of which is stressed. He used rising feet 'as being commonest in English verse,' that is, one consisting of a monosyllable, an iamb, an anapaest, or a fourth paeon (three unstressed syllables preceding a stressed one: ◡ ◡ ◡ —). The time element determines the length of the foot. He looked upon the metrical foot much as a musician would look upon a musical bar. Every bar is of equal length although it may contain one or a number of notes. He thought, however, that in music the time element was too rigid, in poetry not rigid enough.[1] The distinctive feature of the rhythm used by Hopkins is the juxtaposition of strong stresses without syllables between to produce an abrupt effect, that of good prose. Why, he asked, if it is forcible to say 'láshed:ród' in prose must he be obliged 'to weaken this in verse, which ought to be stronger, not weaker, into "láshed birch-ród" or something?' Neither Shakespeare nor Milton weakened his verses by slavishly following a regular scansion. Why should he? The opening of his 'Spring' is an excellent example of this practice. It contains five stresses but only nine syllables—'Nothing is so beautiful as spring.' In lyric verse he liked the scanning to run on from line to line to the end of the stanza. Forgetting the technical details and scanning according to the natural prose stress one finds that the poems fall into groups regularly containing lines of three, four, five, and six stresses, except, of course, for the few poems in a more elaborate pattern. Five stresses is the most usual number. If one reads the poems aloud *making the sense apparent*, he will find that the scansion is not anarchic.

A reader accustomed to present-day poetry will not have the difficulty in understanding Hopkins that Bridges had. He will discount most of Bridges' notes on the poet's faults. Not that those faults do not exist, but the corpus of work free from those blemishes is great enough not to affect his reputation.

[1]It is interesting to note that even here Hopkins anticipated the practice of several contemporary composers. Palmgren in his 'Bird Song' and Mompou in his 'Scenes d'Enfants' attempt to break the rigid pattern by not dividing the score into traditional bars.

The author of *The Testament of Beauty* is not the best guide to a poet such as Hopkins.

One cannot always read Hopkins, especially certain of the poems, nor should he attempt to do so. Hopkins could not even do it himself. To get the most from him, as I have said repeatedly, one must be willing to give one's full attention to the poems. One never reads Hopkins rapidly. He must be read slowly and repeatedly. One must taste and roll on the tongue phrase after phrase as Keats enjoyed doing with claret, and the result is as satisfying. He cannot be gulped. If one is willing to approach the work in this manner he will be abundantly satisfied. Sensuous beauty, exquisite music, a strong masculine tenderness and deep passionate feeling sometimes tragic in its quality, a sensitivity approaching hyper-sensitivity, sorrow for man's defection from the Christlike ideal, and his own loyalty to his ideals are all there. The faults are only the small bits of cork that sometimes get into a glass of wine. I have not called particular attention to them because others have already overstressed them.

Much yet remains to be written about Hopkins. The literary criticism in his letters and notebooks throws much light on his practice as a poet, and reveals his directness and unerring aim in penetrating the vulnerable spots of his fellow poets and of his own. He gave praise where he felt praise was due. He will never be a popular poet. He cannot be, because he makes too many demands on the reader. Among those who do not think deep feeling and intellectual exercise are incompatible, he will long be cherished. They will rank him as a major poet.

AGE and WILLIAM BUTLER YEATS

THE recent death of William Butler Yeats in his seventy-fourth year marks the loss of a major poet who for more than fifty years has published poetry of a sustained high quality. Other poets have lived longer or have had a more extended period of production, but of few can it be said, as it can be said of him, that we would not wish the work of any one period forgotten. Too often a poet tries to repeat in his later years the successes of his youth. The poetry of Mr Yeats, however, in form as well as content, changed as his attitude towards life changed. In the early work there was lushness, sweetness, and a corresponding softness in the rhythms. As he grew older the subject matter steadily grew closer to reality, the rhythms became less tenuous, and the general structure more firm. Perhaps in no phase of his work are these changes reflected more clearly than in those poems dealing with age and its accompaniments: nostalgia for a better day, disillusionment, mutability, ambition and achievement, loss of ardour, wisdom and death.

The young bride in *The Land of Heart's Desire* wishing to remain carefree feared four things: only one, 'drowsy love,' pertained to youth; three—a tongue 'too crafty and too wise,' one 'too godly and too grave,' and one 'more bitter than the tide'—pertained to old age. Those lines, written in youth, reflect a young person's attitude, an attitude which Yeats later found to be essentially untrue.

Poems on nostalgic themes, found in the early as well as the later poems, chart the course from romanticism to reality. 'The Meditation of the Old Fisherman,' published at twenty-four, depicts an old fisherman looking with longing to his youth when the waves were gayer, the herring more plentiful, and the girls more beautiful. Romanticism is instinct in the poignant note of the refrain 'When I was a boy with never a crack in my heart.' Nor would one expect to find a radically different attitude in 'The Old Men Admiring Themselves in the Water' published at thirty-nine. The rhythms, it is true, are less obvious. Instead of slowing the pace by the device used in 'The Lake Isle of Innisfree' and 'When You are Old'—frequent repetition of 'and' with a wealth of liquids and nasals—he creates the sense of a falling away in the rhythm itself (the liquids are still numerous):

> I heard the old, old men say,
> 'All that's beautiful drifts away
> Like the waters.'

At forty-nine, however, he began to realize the changes that life actually brought, changes typified by the alteration in woman's beauty. A melancholy, tender romanticism pervades this theme in the early 'When You Are Old.' Not until 'Fallen Majesty' does it become clear that the expression is more than an imaginative exercise of a talented youth. We know then that the woman that 'seemed a burning cloud' also had blood in her veins. 'Her Praise,' 'His Phoenix,' 'A Deep Sworn Vow,' and 'Broken Dreams' intensify his awareness of the change. 'Her Praise,' for example, narrates the attempt of the poet to talk of the woman with everyone he encountered; each turned the conversation to his own interest. Finally, he determined to seek out some beggar, manœuvre the conversation until it turned upon her, then

> If there be rags enough he will know her name
> And be well pleased remembering it, for in the old days
> Though she had young men's praise and old men's blame,
> Among the poor both old and young gave her praise.

He achieved the same effect in 'His Phoenix' by the use of the refrain, 'I knew a phoenix in my youth, so let them have their day.' In 'A Deep Sworn Vow' he made her his Cynara. Great changes came also to his male friends. Many 'discoverers of forgotten truth' or mere companions of his early days had died, among them Lionel Johnson, George Pollexfen, Major Robert Gregory (who 'had the intensity to have published all to be a world's delight') and John Synge (whom he praised in many poems), all at some time or other visitors at Coole Park, whose hostess possessed the rare ability of bringing out the best in everyone.

At Coole Park, in fact, he became increasingly aware of the changes wrought by time. What great changes when compared with the wild swans which he had watched for nineteen years at Coole!

> Unwearied still, lover by lover
> They paddle in the cold
> Companionable streams or climb the air;
>
> Their hearts have not grown old;
> Passion or conquest, wander where they will,
> Attend upon them still.

The nostalgia imagined in the early poems did materialize, but the poet's communication of the actual experience lacks the softness of the earlier expression. The later poems possess the strength of reality rather than the effeminacy of a too highly sensitized aestheticism.

The septuagenarian's attitude is instinct in 'Beautiful Lofty Things' and 'The Municipal Gallery Re-Visited.' The companions of his middle years had become Olympians—'a thing never known again.' No one, wrote Yeats, could have a true estimate of him from his work only; he must look beyond that to the friends he had and realize that 'most begins and ends' with his friends. Not only did Mr Yeats believe that certain of them surpassed any of the present generation—the members of which were more shadowy to him than they—but he believed that the present generation marked a deterioration in mankind.

He expressed this sentiment as early as 1914 in 'To A Child
Dancing in the Wind.' A much deeper disillusionment, however, came in 1919 when he discovered that all he and his
friends had done for peace and other humane causes had come
to nought. An equally great sense of disillusionment pervades
the poems published in 1938.

Man now stands, he wrote in his last volume of poems,
ready to rend his fellow man, a 'gracious time' has given way
to one where 'conduct and work grow coarse, and coarse the
soul,' where statesmen and journalists lie glibly, where folly is
linked with elegance, where actors have no sense of music. But,
from the 'dark betwixt the polecat and the owl' he foresaw that
a new order of 'workman, noble and saint' would arise. He saw
the world, in other words, much as do his younger contemporaries—Day Lewis, Auden, and Spender.

Between youth, that notorious waster of beauty, and age
which resigns itself to the truth that the beauty of which it
dreamed in earlier years is but transient, stands the man in his
late forties and early fifties, rebellious at what he already dimly
perceives to be the truth. He would warn the incredulous
spendthrifts of the many things he had learned from experience. But the gulf is unbridgeable. In 'Two Years Later,' 'The
Living Beauty,' 'A Song,' and 'Shepherd and Goatherd' Mr
Yeats gave expression to this age-old condition. Exasperation
at the inability of youth to learn from the experiences of their
elders pervades the first. When has there ever been a youth
'who could have foretold that the heart grows old!' Because
older men cannot pay to living beauty 'its tribute of wild tears,'
they should content themselves with beauty cast from bronze
or chiselled from marble. Of necessity, youth, the exponent of
the 'natural life,' must always differ from age, whose life is
compounded of sterner stuff. Only the older men, learned in
patience, are able to measure out the road trod by the soul.
Youth is too impatient to show whatever it has found.

The publication in his forty-fifth year of *The Green Helmet*

and Other Poems was a milestone in Mr Yeats' poetic career.
Until that time he had been chiefly concerned in 'rhyming his
reveries.' The new and all later volumes attest an increasing
attention to the problem of wisdom. Careful readers have always been aware of this change, but too many anthologists,
unfortunately, have continued to stress the early work. It is
significant that when Mr Yeats selected for the *Oxford Book of
Modern Verse* those poems of his by which he wished to be
represented none is from an early period. He must have realized that in spite of their value as poetic achievements, he did
not know what he was talking about when he wrote them. At
forty-five he thought he could speak of wisdom coming with
age—that he could 'wither into the truth.' But at seventy-three
truth had not yet come. Between these two ages lies Mr Yeats'
greatest poetry.

At least three women played an important part in shaping
him: one, a sympathetic companion, provided a union of
minds; a second unbound from him 'youth's dreamy load' until she so changed him that he lived 'labouring in ecstasy'; the
third, though possibly unworthy, stirred his passions so deeply
that only to think of her at a later time suffused him with a
sweetness so great that he shook from head to foot.

'An Irish Airman Foresees his Death' is a clear statement of
an older attitude. The airman was not deluded into a hatred towards those against whom he was fighting, nor into a love for
those whom he guarded. He chose his career as a result of 'a
lonely impulse of delight' when, on balancing everything, both
the future and the past seemed a waste of breath compared to
the present moment—'this life, this death.' Wisdom, he believed, did not lie in logic. As the protagonist in 'Tom
O'Roughley' said, 'Wisdom is a butterfly and not a gloomy
bird of prey.' Nor should a person concern himself unduly with
death; what is it but a second wind? The poet even became
sceptical as to whether or not improvement comes with the
years. He liked to delude himself into thinking that the reason

a woman's beauty no longer moved him as it would have done in his youth was that he had become wise; but it was probably little more than mere rationalization:

> But I grow old among dreams,
> A weather-worn marble triton
> Among the streams.

The really magnificent poem, 'A Prayer for My Daughter,' clearly marks the change in values that had come with the years. True it is that he wished his daughter to be beautiful, but not a ravishing beauty. More important for her were courtesy, graciousness, a mind free from hatred and envy, a self-delighting soul, and a husband with a proper esteem for tradition and ceremony—

> Ceremony's a name for the rich born,
> And custom for the spreading laurel tree.

The difference between the music of Mr Yeats' early and later poetry is as great as that between the poems of Milton's early period and that of *Paradise Lost* and *Samson Agonistes*, and points in the same direction. With the publication of *The Tower* (1928) the music assumes a stateliness—until that time but dimly foreshadowed—that suits the more thoughtful tone of the subject matter and the greater experience of the poet. It is not less warm than the early work; it burns with a deeper fire. It is often difficult, but never vague. The rhythms are tighter; the imagery, more subtle.

At sixty-two the poet had come to realize that the land of youth was not for him—that land of passion where

> Caught in that sensual music all neglect
> Monuments of unaging intellect——

He must sail to Byzantium to learn how the soul grows from experience and study of the ancient monuments of wisdom—and there

Consume my heart away; sick with desire
And fastened to a dying animal
It knows not what it is; and gather me
Into the artifice of eternity.

He rebelliously accepted the realization of what he must do. A
general feeling of rebellion also permeates the first section of
'The Tower.' 'This absurdity'—decrepit age—had been tied to
him 'as to a dog's tail.' Never had he experienced the intensity
of excitement, passion, imagination, as at the present, and yet
he must bid the Muse go back and study the philosophers until he
could deal in abstract things 'or be derided by a sort of battered
kettle at the heel.' The revolt is particularized in section ii and
admirably caught in the rhythmical structure of the verse. In
section iii, however, the music becomes bold and courageous,
reflecting the change of mood from revolt to one of pride and
courage. It was time, he said, to write his will; to upstanding
men of action he left his pride and faith while he in his old age
disciplines his soul at Byzantium until those things which
bring sorrow and disappointment lose their immediacy—

Seem but the clouds of the sky
When the horizon fades;
Or the bird's sleepy cry
Among the deepening shades.

Revolt and doubt also appear when he is among school children who make him painfully aware of his age. Could any
mother—could she envisage the child as a man of sixty—think
the trouble of bearing children worth while? From this thought,
however, he passes to the greater question of man's attempt to
solve the problem of self, and incidentally, that of God. He but
poses the question in the last stanza of 'Among School Children'; he attempts no answer. The only real enemy of man is
time.
At sixty-seven the poet believed he had discovered certain

truths that would aid others. After forty, for example, a man must examine carefully the things he does and call all things extravagant

> That are not suited for such men as come
> Proud, open-eyed and laughing to the tomb.

But at fifty a man can still be capable of a rapture so great that he can be blessed and can bless. Age brought, however, a burden of responsibility which weighed the poet down—a responsibility for things said or not said in days long past which appalled his conscience or his vanity. Two things, however, became constantly clearer to him as he grew older—the futility of remorse and the value of experience. He could review the period of the ignominy of boyhood, the distress of boyhood changing into man, man's awareness of his bungling, the malice of enemies, all—and yet could forgive himself, because when he cast out remorse a great sweetness suffused him; his heart was filled with the same type of happiness that he could feel at fifty and even younger.

Reluctantly the poet gradually accepted what man has been told by Sophocles, by the great Elizabethans, by Goethe, and by innumerable others—that we can never achieve true wisdom. At seventy-three he could write:

> My temptation is quiet.
> Here at life's end
> Neither loose imagination,
> Nor the mill of the mind
> Consuming its rag and bone,
> Can make the truth known.

For Yeats it became the 'property of the dead, a something incompatible with life'; the living only had power. The soul might say, 'Seek out reality'; but the heart takes a different attitude. Since no one is able personally to experience all that time has denied to lovers, an old man, just as youth, can find

peace by thinking that in himself are atoms of the world soul—
that in his veins there are kings as well as beggars. Mr Yeats
sometimes had moods, it is true, in which he believed he had
achieved wisdom. He stated it ironically in 'After Long
Silence':

> Bodily decrepitude is wisdom young;
> We loved each other and were ignorant.

It interested him to think not only that in his youth he had
often been 'mad as the mist and snow,' but that such authors
as Horace, Plato, 'many-minded Homer,' and even Cicero
had also had similar moments in their youth and early manhood.

Old age was not, however, without its advantages. It
brought freedom from the necessity of pretence, which en-
abled him to say:

> I carry the sun in a golden cup,
> The moon in a silver bag;

and it brought freedom of speech. Old persons could talk
about and admit earlier happenings that they would never
dared to have talked about at the time.

Authorship has always worn for the layman a cloak of
mystery. He is interested, therefore, when an author removes
the cloak and gives him an insight into his calling. Mr Yeats
has given us not one, but many such glimpses. He expressed
the youthful attitude in 'To Ireland in the Coming Times,' a
poem with a masculine quality of frankness, energy, boldness
and control. The thoughtful reader, he said, will discover that
his rhymes 'more than their rhyming tell of things discovered
in the deep.' That Yeats was a careful craftsman is everywhere
evident in his work. But few realize the labour necessary to
achieve one beautiful line of poetry, especially since the result
must appear to be spontaneous. But, as he has told us in
'Adam's Curse,' as in poetry, so is it in all things; 'we must

labour to be beautiful,' even with love. As he admonished a fellow artist, discrimination was necessary in all things, particularly in the companions one chooses. He had disciplined himself to the degree that he could say:

> There is not a fool can call me friend,
> And I may dine at journey's end
> With Landor and with Donne.
>
> ('To a Young Beauty') aet. 53

Yeats was just as aware of the changes in his poetry as is the most careful reader. The creatures of his youthful fancy and imagination—witches, centaurs, etc.—had vanished, and at fifty he was left with cold reality and was forced to 'endure the timid sun.' But he never minimized the cost of creation, regardless of the field of activity. 'Whatever flames upon the night,' he wrote at sixty-one, 'man's own resinous heart has fed.' He called himself the last of those romantics who had chosen for their themes 'traditional sanctity and loveliness' and all that most could bless 'the mind of man or elevate a rhyme.' But he believed those times had gone leaving a world of darkness and confusion. No longer did the high horse of poetry have a rider. What poetry there is, however, can give a keen delight; the delight of the rattle of pebbles on the shore under the receding wave.

Mr Yeats would have been unusual had he not suffered his moments of grave doubt as to his wisdom in devoting his life to poetry. 'The Choice' crystallizes his doubt. Man is faced with a choice of making either his life or his work perfection; he cannot have both. If he chooses the latter, as he did, even though he gains success, the toil has not only left its mark, but he still endured that 'old perplexity an empty purse, or the day's vanity, the night's remorse.' To those who would object to the earthiness of his later poems, Mr Yeats had but one answer, 'The Spur.' What else is left to an old man as a spur to song but lust and rage! At the close of his life he realized that although he had attempted to fulfil the promise of his youth he had not found complete satisfaction. His demon, 'Plato's ghost,' constantly goaded him to new goals by asking as soon as one was reached, 'What then?' From 'Are You Content?' published at seventy-three, we learn that he had come to believe that only the dead could judge a poet's accomplishment— certainly, he could not.

In numerous other ways Mr Yeats' later poetry differs from the earlier. 'A Last Confession' from 'A Woman Young and Old' differs from what would have been his treatment of this subject in his earlier years. Youth would be incredulous of its 'earthiness,' just as it might be toward poems like 'A Drunken Man's Praise of Sobriety.' No young poet would use the imagery that Yeats, at sixty-six, used in 'Lullaby.' The music has a strong, masculine beauty, but the images of Paris, Tristram, and Zeus and Leda are not the ones usually associated with innocence.

The difference between the early and late work is clearly epitomized in the poems on death. The description of the death of the old foxhunter in 'The Ballad of the Foxhunter' is clearly as a youth of twenty-four would imagine it—tender, gentle, melancholy, languorous with a mixture of fortitude— qualities vividly reflected in the music of the verse—

> His eyelids droop, his head falls low,
> His old eyes cloud with dreams;
> The sun upon all things that grow
> Falls in sleepy streams.

At sixty-four in 'Spilt Milk' the romantic characteristics have vanished, the expression approaches the matter-of-fact:

> We that have done and thought,
> That have thought and done,
> Must ramble, and thin out
> Like milk spilt on a stone.

No amount of questioning on death, he wrote in 'At Algeciras'

brought him a solution which he could utter with confidence.
The sum of his wisdom is best expressed in 'An Acre of Grass,'
one stanza of which I have already quoted, and in the final
stanzas of 'The Wild Old Wicked Man':

> 'All men live in suffering
> I know as few can know,
> Whether they take the upper road
> Or stay content on the low,
> Rower bent in his row-boat
> Or weaver bent at his loom,
> Horseman erect upon horseback
> Or child hid in the womb.'
>
> Day-break and a candle end.

> 'That some stream of lightning
> From the old man in the skies
> Can burn out that suffering
> No right-taught man denies.
> But a coarse old man am I,
> I choose the second-best,
> I forget it all while
> Upon a woman's breast.'
>
> Day-break and a candle end.

What is true of the poems dealing with age and its accompaniments is equally true of all of the subjects treated by Mr
Yeats. He attempted in his early poetry to mingle the music of
Spenser and Shelley in order to make a style which would be
musical and full of colour, a style, he wrote at thirty-six, 'from
which others would catch fire.' The result would be a really
great school of ballad poetry in Ireland. When he realized that
his poetry was 'too full of the reds and yellows Shelley gathered
in Italy,' he attempted to set things right 'by eating little and
sleeping upon a board.' Later, he adopted a more practical
plan. He made his rhythms more faint and nervous and filled

his images with a 'a certain coldness, a certain wintry wildness.' After his fortieth year his poetry became increasingly thoughtful and the music infinitely more subtle. The earthiness of many of his poems—some would prefer to call it their paganism—is in startling contrast to the nostalgic youthful melancholy of the earlier work. But in the earlier as well as the later volumes one necessarily realizes that the thought, rhythm, word, and image are inextricably bound together. Modern English poetry has lost its last great practitioner.

LAURENCE BINYON

OVER forty years ago Mr Laurence Binyon published his first volume of poems. Since that time few years have elapsed in which he has not given us of his store—poetry, plays, and latterly, appreciations on both oriental and occidental art. He has found time for all this in spite of a busy life at the British Museum. He first lectured in America in 1912, repeating his visits in 1914, 1926 and 1933. It is unfortunate for Mr Binyon that he is known to the average reader by his war poems, many of which have already begun to date. There is so much else (of an enduring quality) in his poetry to support us in this seemingly chaotic world. He is distinctively a contemporary poet in that his poetry is his reactions—those of a thoughtful, reflective, sensitive, and courageous man—to the environment of contemporary life. His imagination has been affected by the spiritual and material conditions of the day.

In contrast to the poetry of Mr T. S. Eliot Mr Binyon affects a reconstruction of beauty against the forces of disintegration—forces against which Mr Eliot seems powerless to act. Mr Eliot's poetry is a balm to the contemporary who lacks the strength to combat the anti-cultural forces of the present day. Mr Binyon's poetry is a constant challenge to a fuller life. He sees that in spite of the apparent chaos of twentieth century civilization, beauty, serenity, and the abundant life are still attainable. This idea is clearly stated in the early volumes written before the war, and is as unmistakable and more firmly presented in those written since. I am not concerned in this essay in commenting on the weaknesses of Mr Binyon's poetry—and there are weaknesses of such magnitude that when we lay aside the volumes we feel that we have been in the presence of a great poet but only occasionally in the presence of great poetry: weaknesses chiefly attributable to lack of condensation and excision. But I wish rather to attempt a synthesis of Mr

Binyon's poetic thought, because it is the product of a man who has touched life—not drawn away in a feeling of revulsion—and has found it worth while. Life has repaid his courage. When viewed chronologically, a steady growth—at least a constant ripening process—can be seen in his poetry. The fundamental tenets of his philosophy remain unchanged, but those tenets become more subtle with the accretion of years.

I

There is a fundamental unity of idea which links the poems: it is an adventure of the mind seeking the release of the soul. Although Mr Binyon is a poet content to work in the great tradition of English poetry with which he is thoroughly imbued, he does not look to the past either as a means of escape from the present or as a period when life was better than it now is. He is content to shoulder the responsibilities of the present. There is the same courage manifest in his work as in that of A. E. Housman. Mr Eliot tells us in his essay 'The Function of Criticism' that 'between the true artists of any time there is . . . an unconscious community.' That, of course, is not original with Mr Eliot. In 1817, Shelley stated the idea fully and definitely in the preface to 'The Revolt of Islam.' 'There must be a resemblance,' he wrote, 'which does not depend upon their own will, between all the writers of any particular age. They cannot escape from subjection to a common influence which arises out of an infinite combination of circumstances belonging to the times in which they live; though each is in a degree the author of the very influence by which his being is thus pervaded.' Mr Eliot limits this community of ideas to the first-rate artists. Here, I believe, he errs, because it is just because the great bulk of our present day literature—'blotterature' is the term John Colet used for it in 1512—contains only the current ideas, that it lives but for the moment. Shelley wisely included 'all the writers.'

I have suggested that many of the poems appear to be linked by a common subject. This is true; but in no poem is the subject fully stated. I do not mean that each poem is not complete in itself, but rather to suggest that in order to arrive at an adequate understanding of the whole corpus of Mr Binyon's thought we must acquaint ourselves with more than a few poems. He is not an ascetic nor is he the advocate of ascetism. He keeps near life. He enunciates his main idea in 'Porphyrion' (which could with profit be compared with Shelley's 'Alastor'), clothes it in modern garb in 'The Supper,' augments it in 'The Renewal,' restates the theme with variations in several poems from *Auguries* (particularly 'The Tiger Lily'), *The Four Years*, and other volumes, and makes a *rifacimento* in the prelude to 'The Sirens.' The development of the theme is rich and harmonious. All Mr Binyon's poetry fits into his philosophy of life which can be briefly stated as follows—providing, of course, that we make due allowance for the suggestive quality of his language: Happiness and a sense of the completeness of life can belong only to the person of great humanity, the prime requisite for which is an all-comprehending love achieved by a close and sympathetic contact with one's fellows. The timid and weak remain shut out from this happiness because they lack the courage necessary for such a life; without courage, integrity, and will, advance is impossible. The love of humanity is not a theoretic love divorced from the love of the individual, but rather, one might say, is one of the results of personal love. At least they are mutually helpful. Mr Binyon's merit lies in his individual treatment of the component parts of the foregoing theme. It is clear that he is a democrat of the finest type. Let us examine his poetry with these ideas in mind, beginning with 'The Supper' in which both the negative and positive elements are set before the reader in unmistakable terms.

A rich youth accustomed to luxury, dissatisfied with life, and vaguely aware that without humanity and love for his fellows life is incomplete, seizes the idea that he can secure happiness

by raising out of their pain some unfortunates from the street.
. . . Accordingly, he brings to his table a blind beggar, a sand-
wichman, a tramp, two women, and a thief who try to be gay
at a banquet which he has prepared. Instead of his bringing
comfort to them, however, they bring unhappiness to him by
forcing him to look into his own soul. In his toast, the tramp
Michael introduces the note of the uncertainty of worldly possessions and the meaninglessness of the mere acquisition.
Michael pledges the host's health:

> I drink your good health but be sure of the end.
> You never can tell you won't come to the cold,
> And the bed from under your body be sold.
> You smile at your ease; you pay no heed:
> You think to lay hands on all that you need,
> And still you go piling your riches high;
> But where is the use of it all, say I?

The young host, however, like many in his position, listens
politely but unmoved, and apologizes lamely for his sheltered
existence in a patronizing tone:

> Well said, my friend: you've a heart in your breast;
> And a brave heart beating is worth all the rest.
> Where is the use of it all? 'Tis true:
> But we walk in the way we're accustomed to.

Since it takes courage to lift oneself out of a rut the majority
emulate the young host even though they know that by doing
so they are denied the happiness that comes from a full life.

In spite of their desire for happiness an unrest seizes the
guests as they sit at the table. Annie, the unfortunate, expresses
the subconscious feeling of each. In the midst of life on the
street, the fatigue, the pain, the grief, the fear—all are alleviated.
There is a fulness which makes them oblivious of self in the
knowledge of being a part of a greater whole. But in the quiet-
ness of the room their individual ills assume the ascendancy.
Puzzled, Annie muses:

I know not how, but down in the street
'Tis not so heavy a task to meet.
A power beyond me bears me along,
The faint with the eager, the weak with the strong.
'Tis like an army with marching sound;
I march, and my feet forget the ground.
I have no thought, no wish, no fear;
And the others are brave for me. But here,
I know not why, I long to rest;
I have an aching in my breast.
O I am tired! how sweet 'twould be
To yield, to struggle no more, and be free!

A chance remark, reawakening in her the remembrance of her
earlier life and causing her to suffer again her individual tragedy, arouses her to anger, and in despair she seeks relief in the
crowded streets. Unrest is likewise sown in the hearts of the
other guests who in turn revile their host. The shallowness of
his humanity is revealed in his pique against them and his weak
defence that he pitied them. Averill, the sandwich-man, replies
that pity is all right, 'but it will not hold men up from hell.' He
and his companions are Necessity's children and her mark is
ever on them. When she calls, says Averill,

We must not tarry.
We must take up our yoke again,
With labouring feet for ever
To follow her triumph's train

To follow her sleepless course.
And to fall when she decrees
With wailing that no man hearkens,
With tramplings that no man sees.

He who will help them out of the slough and assist them in
setting their feet in the way to follow their far desire must be a

man of courage, a man who knows that there is no 'relish keener than the pang of useless pain' and 'no spice more rare' than that rained by tears of wisdom.

This idea of being Necessity's children recalls Godwin's *Political Justice* and its chapter on Necessity. It is an idea which appeals generally to young people and to those not strong enough to buck the current of circumstance and environment. Wordsworth eagerly embraced the doctrine in his youth but later discarded it. The facile critic who tosses it lightly aside does not as a rule consider deeply enough the influences of heredity and environment. On the other hand, he who embraces it whole-heartedly overlooks certain inherent characteristics of man's nature. For poetical purposes, however, there is no need to cavil at the idea.

Averill invites the young host to 'eat of the mad desire,' the terrors that haunt them, the torment that will not let them die, all the experiences of life—which result in wisdom. But the host, lacking the courage to live, is unable to accept Averill's invitation—Averill the young poet who knows life: Averill who is Binyon or what Binyon might wish to be. 'I thought that I could love my kind!' mutters the host to himself when alone, his head buried in his hands:

> Love is vast, and I was blind.
> O mighty world, my weakness spare!
> This love is more than I can dare.

The theme that happiness, or at least satisfaction, can come only to those who have the courage to drink deeply of life is not a new one. It is a favourite subject with poets who give to it their individual touch. Wordsworth's 'Lines written on a Seat under a Yew Tree' is only one example.

But what can this Necessity about which Averill speaks do? To the man of courage who flings wide his arms in eager expectation it can bring the 'lovely joy' that rises from the transmutation of all experiences. He who does not play the

game of evasion will feel as he delves deeper into life his own
life 'open like a flower' within him.

II

I have dealt at thus great length with this early poem because it contains many of the phases of Mr Binyon's attitude
towards life. The poem is the impassioned expression of a
youth filled with noble aims. The language is simple and clear
and points very definitely the course Mr Binyon's later poetry
is to follow: the thought deepens, the expression becomes
subtilized and concentrated, the prosody less facile but more
flexible. We can compare him to a young tennis player full of
fire and speed but not yet mature in his generalship; the later
work loses some of the youthful spontaneity but gains from
better judgment, a keener eye, and richer experience. And like
a tennis player, too, he has his off moments when he misses,
but these we must overlook and remember, instead, the numerous times when he rouses enthusiasm by his brilliant strokes.

In the prelude to 'The Sirens'—one of Mr Binyon's later
works—it is not difficult to imagine that it is Averill of 'The
Supper'—Averill grown older—who sings

... the flesh is no longer a home, nor can comforting Earth
Shelter me more.
I am known to the Unknown, chosen, charmed, endangered:
I flow to a music ocean-wild and starry,
And feel within me, for this mortality's answer,
Sea without shore.

Of course this plunge into the stream of life exacts a great
toll, and a regenerating influence is frequently necessary. What
is the source of this influence? Certainly not in the sheltered
room of the young host! But rather it is found where Wordsworth found it: in nature in all her manifestations, but more
particularly in the sunlight. The young poet of 'The Renewal'

shows himself as ardent a sun-worshipper as the enthusiastic youth of to-day. 'I need,' he cries,

> I need each beam of the young sun; I need
> Each draught of the pure wind, whereon to feed
> My joy; each sparkle of the dew that shines
> Under your branches, dark, sun-drunken pines.
> All voices, motions of the unwearied sea;
> But most, O tender spirit,[1] I need thee.

The courageous youth, realizing his affinity to him who lifted a moment on the waves has a sudden glimpse of boundless skies, exclaims in a passage strongly recalling the phraseology of Shelley and Keats:

> Now is mere breathing joy; and all that strife
> Confused and darkling, that we miscall life
> Is as a cloak, cast off in the warm spring.
> Thus to possess the sunlight, is a thing
> Worth more than our ambitions; more than ease
> Wrung from the despot labour, the stale lees
> Of youthful bliss . . .
> And, O more precious even yet than this,
> Empowers our weakness to support in bliss
> The immensity of love, to love in vain
> Yet still to hunger for that priceless pain;
> To love without a bound, to set no end
> To our long love, never aside to bend
> In loving, but pour forth in living streams
> Our hearts, as the full morn in quenchless beams.
> He that this light has tasted, asks no more
> Dim questions answerless, that have so sore
> Perplexed our thinking: in his bosom flow
> Springs of all knowledge he hath need to know.

It is interesting to note in passing that Mr Eliot exhibits none

[1]The sun.

of this love for, or dependence on nature which looms so largely in Mr Binyon's work.

How is one to achieve this great experience without which life is only half lived? The answer is scattered among many of Mr Binyon's shorter poems. He must possess integrity of mind and action. He must divest himself of the thoughts that are not his and of beliefs which he affirms but which his deeper consciousness cannot accept, because such are of death—the death that has no aim. The lover—and we have seen how much is required of him—is 'always young and wise' ('The Snows of Spring'). Not 'Earth's sad bondage, nor pious walls of Time, nor the gates of Death' hold any fears for him, because, sings the poet in rapturous lines:

> For the marvel that was most marvellous is most true;
> To the music that moves the universe moves my heart,
> And the song of the starry worlds I sing apart
> In the night and shadow and stillness, Love, for you.
>   ('A Hymn of Love')

I have said that courage is a constant note in Mr Binyon's poetry. To the man who lacks it, he tells us in 'Santa Christina,'

> Dark is the world to the weak will
> As to feet stumbling on a hill
> Benighted, when no stars appear,

but to the possessor, and especially in young and frail bodies is the beauty of courage 'seen and sung.'

> There, like a fountain ever new,
> Thou dost scatter sunny dew,
> Troubling our self-bewildered night
> With simplicity of light.

In 'Sorrow,' Mr Binyon elaborates the idea of the necessity for an all-comprehending humanity. It is worthwhile quoting the poem for the greater clarity it gives to his poetic ideas:

Woe to him that has not known the woe of man,
Who has not felt within him burning all the want
Of desolated bosoms, since the world began,
Felt, as his own, the burden of the fears that daunt;
Who has not eaten failure's bitter bread, and been
Among those ghosts of hope that haunt the day, unseen.

Only when we are hurt with all the hurt untold,—
In us the thirst, the hunger, and ours the helpless hands,
The palsied effort vain, the darkness and the cold,—
Then, only then, the Spirit knows and understands,
And finds in every sigh breathed out beneath the sun
The human heart that makes us infinitely one.

Elsewhere he tells us that he who would know the mystery of the world must search 'those deep regions . . . where lives are herded, ignorant what they are,' and must put on 'their being . . . if [he] would know humanity' ('The Renewal'); he must search the world 'whose wrong Mocks holy beauty and our desire' ('A Vision of Resurrection'), aware that 'life is all a cheapening And the Rain is over everything, And there is neither mirth nor woe' ('The Tram'), yet he must never lose sight of the gleam however hard beset by the question of responsibility, 'Who made it so, who made it so?'

The way is not always smooth even for the courageous. There are times when, still desiring to forge ahead, we are daunted by the world which seems to come 'as an army against us.' When such happens who has not longed then 'for a strength past pain To endure the rending of sorrow that makes hope vain, To be kneaded in iron and stubborned in armour of stone' ('Auguries VIII')? Mr Binyon recognizes that once a person has undergone a purification of his dross through the agency of the sharp realities of life, be it in peace or war, he is ever more eager to fulfil his high destiny in life:

> . . . if torn and bruised
> The heart, more urgent comes our cry
> Brain, sinew, and spirit, before we die.
> Beat out the iron, edge it keen,
> And shape us to the end we mean!
>
> ('The Anvil')

> I find for my thought not a close,
>   For my soul not an end,
> With you[1] will I follow, nor crave
>   the strength of the strong
> Nor a fortress of time to enshield me
>   from storms that rend.
> This is life, this is home, to be poured
>   as a stream, as a song.
>
> ('Auguries XI')

If we link certain lines of 'Past and Future' in which the poet tells us that we are unable to foresee the effects of our acts upon others; and that even our most insignificant deeds often have such far-reaching results that when instead of their influence ending it is just beginning—if, I say, we link those lines with the fore-going, we have one conception of immortality. Our immortality depends on the influence we exert on others, and every person exerts some kind of influence, good or bad. There is sufficient justification for living as fine lives as we are able if by doing so we are raising the standards of the world. It is as if each of us were a drop of water from a full vessel. By our worthy actions in this world the drop representing us is purified, and when it is reabsorbed into the full vessel the whole will be affected slightly. This is not quite the same thing as the general soul about which Tennyson speaks in 'In Memoriam.' In the beautiful but uneven 'The Mirror II,' Mr Binyon throws additional light on this subject. The soul cries:

[1] O waters swift.

I that am want, I that am grief,
I that am love, I that am mirth,
I that am fear, I that am fire,
Though thou clothe me in beauty brief,
Though I have worn thy sweet attire,
I, thy endless sorrow, Earth,
Dwell in the glory of God's desire,
That kneads forever in the flesh
Of man, to make his spirit afresh,
A marvel more than all the wandering seas
And mightier than thy caverned mysteries,
Nor stays nor sleeps, but world on world transfuses
Melted ever to diviner uses,
Through infinite swift changes burning,
Itself the end, no end discerning,
Till all the universe be wrought
Into its far perfecting thought.
Then this mind of cloud and rue
Shall in eternal mind be new,
Mirror of God, pure and alone,
See and be seen, know and be known.

The aim of the soul is its constant striving towards perfection. Of course, the poet tells us, no man has ever seen his soul except for a brief glimpse in the night. To see it as it really is 'eternity must enter him.' Mr Binyon's thought is inseparable from his diction and any attempt at separation results but in a partial truth. Through the suggestive powers of his language he helps us to extend our vision.

Love—we should remember that to our poet 'light, life, and love' are one—is one of the most potent means for uplifting the soul. In many lyrics of surpassing beauty and tenderness the purifying influence of love is presented to us. In 'Parting and Meeting,' 'Day's End,' and 'The Crucible' he reveals how, because love came,

> . . . my soul hath taken wings,
> Newly bathed in light intense.

Only he who has loved deeply can appreciate the sentiment expressed in 'I want a thousand things to-night.'

> Hungers, despairs, and victories,
> And all the world's glories and alarms,
> Forget their wound and find their prize
> But on your lips, but in your arms,

or will agree that

> Life has no more to give than the sweet sound
> Breaking and melting deep in my heart's heart,
>   ('Flowers and Voice')

the sound being his Love's voice uttering 'words of no art' at his knee. Again, he tells us, that truth is found only 'where the heart runs to be poured utterly.' The apotheosis of love is expressed in the final stanza of 'The Crusader.' It is clear, I think, that Mr Binyon is the poet of completion as contrasted with Mr Eliot, the poet of frustration.

III

I have mentioned that in Mr Binyon's poetry nature serves many uses. He is an ardent lover not only of her larger aspects but of her minutiae as well. Because he loves her there is an exciting freshness in his images. He employs her in his poetry in many ways: as a great healer and interpreter of life in such poems as 'The Renewal,' 'The Tiger Lily,' 'The Snows of Spring,' 'Morn like a Thousand Spears'; as a subject for landscape and a setting for love poems in 'Between the mountains and the plain,' 'Ferry Hinksey,' or 'An Hour'; and as embellishment. Frequently use is made of all forms in one poem. His images from the light, the night, and the sea awaken in us the memories of our own experience. In one brief passage he conveys the infinite of the starry sky: 'How huge and still Night sleeps!' . . .

Ten thousand stars through height on height
Burn over us, how breathless and how bright!
Some mild, some fevered, some august and large,
Royal and blazing like a hero's targe,
Some faint and secret, from abysses brought,
Lone as an incommunicable thought !
They throng, they reign, they droop, they bloom, they glow
Upon our gaze, and as we gaze they grow
In patience and in glory, till the mind
Is brimmed and to all other beings blind;
They hang, they fall towards us, spears of fire
Piercing us through with joy and with desire.

('Sirmione')

We feel the salt breeze in our faces as we sit watching

. . . the full waves towering toward the shore,
Heaved up and ever falling in dumb roar,
And snowed into a thousand stormy drops.

('Queen Venus')

And in the exquisite restraint of the 'Lament'—a poem worthy to be placed by the side of 'Rose Aylmer' and 'Requiescat'— the figure of the snow harmonizes beautifully with the character of the thought:

Fall now, my cold thoughts, frozen fall
My sad thoughts, over my heart,
To be the tender burial
Of sweetness and of smart.

Fall soft as snow, when all men sleep,
On copse and on bank forlorn,
That tenderly buries, yet buries deep
Frail violets, freshly born.

There are innumerable sustained similes scattered throughout the poems as well as epithets which remind us that the poet has trained a steady, clear-seeing eye on the objects he describes. There are the 'stubborn arms' and the 'terraced boughs' of the cedars of Lebanon ('The Death of Adam'), the 'little fronds almost uncurled Where still the dead brown bracken's lying' ('The Tram'), the fallen leaf 'fair with rime' on the grey sand path ('The Unreturning Spring'), and Oxford the 'city white with spires' ('Ferry Hinksey'), Mr Binyon is also able to create the mood of a poem and direct the tone of our thoughts by his rare descriptive ability not only of natural phenomena but of the phenomena which are the essence of daily life. The entire poem 'Midsummer Noon,' the monks in 'S. Francesco del Deserto,' the progress of the dray in the poem of the same name, the lush May evening in 'A Hymn of Love,' the children just emerged from the dark, standing dazzled in 'The Belfry,' and the little dancers in the poem of the same name are but a few examples.

I have mentioned that Mr Binyon is well known for his war poems. Save for a very few, I think these poems will date sooner than much of his earlier work. In general, there is neither the clear perspective, nor the depth, nor the recollected passion which we find in his other poems. But in 'Morn like a Thousand Spears,' 'Strike Stone on Steel,' and 'The Unreturning Spring,'—poems which will rank with his finest—the idea expressed is that war is an interlude in the constant search for the fulfilment of life in which man is testing himself. For a moment, man, 'simple and brave . . . the soarer, free of heavens to roam in' who has a world of light in which to home is confounding day with darkness, but only momentarily. Viewed in its place in *The Four Years*, 'The Fallen,' one of Mr Binyon's most popular lyrics, recedes in importance.

Mr Binyon will be classed as a subjective poet (I say with FitzGerald, 'Damn the word!'), but there are poems like the perfect 'The Little Dancers' which are objective. But in using the terms 'subjective' and 'objective' I feel much as FitzGerald did when the terms came into general use almost a hundred years ago. I use them because 'people begin to fancy they understand what [they] mean.' Personally, I know no poet who is wholly one or the other, and any writer who looks as steadily at the object as Mr Binyon does must have much objectivity.

Many divergent tendencies are successfully fused in the poet's work. In the earlier poems the influences are somewhat apparent, just as those in Keats's early work; but in his finest lyrics, again just as in Keats's Odes, the influences are thoroughly assimilated and we have a new voice. Mr Binyon's ultimate position will probably rest on his shorter poems. None of his long ones is wholly successful, yet each reveals the unmistakable characteristics of his finest lyrics. In the earlier poems, Keats of the Odes, Shelley of 'Alastor,' 'Adonais,' and the lyrics, Milton of 'Lycidas,' 'Paradise Lost,' and 'Paradise Regained,' the elegiac quality of Arnold, the meditative quality of Wordsworth, the ecstatic quality of Tennyson's 'Maud,' as well as reminiscences of his contemporaries, are evident; yet in no mere slavish imitation. They are evident because in all sensitive people like Mr Binyon the mind is capable of receiving subtle impressions. At the time he wrote, those impressions were not yet completely absorbed. In his treatment of nature, for example, he could be shown to parallel the methods of such widely divergent writers as Marvell, Vaughan, and Wordsworth. But what would it amount to? Merely that Mr Binyon has felt the divergent tendencies about him. He does not hearken to one voice and only one. Even in the early poems, however, a distinctive note is clearly audible.

In the matter of prosody, too, Mr Binyon has done much experimenting. There are several different tones in his blank verse. His couplets possess freedom and can be either grave or spirited. He can use the strophic form successfully, yet some of his short lyrics in conventional metres are the finest things he has done. There are times, however, when he attempts stanza forms of such complexity that the subject matter cannot stand the strain. His 'To a Summer Night' with its occasional internal rhymes and elaborate form is but one instance. In his later work the structural form becomes freer, the voice surer, and as a result we have such moving poetry as we find in the prelude to 'The Sirens.' In this freer form and in many of the lyrics of conventional mould, Mr Binyon's voice is decidedly worth listening to.

I think it must be generally admitted that in the poems of Mr Binyon we have the proper subject matter for great poetry. The sum total of the effect of his work is greater than that of any single poem, due to the presence of much that is uninspired or at least unsuccessful. There is little 'pure' poetry where the words quiver on the verge of song and where the magic of the arrangement transcends the meaning. In a judicious selection of his work Mr Binyon will appear a greater poet than his complete works will permit us to believe. His genius, like that of most modern poets, reveals itself best in his short lyrics where the tone is always dignified, sometimes elegiac, frequently impassioned, and in a few cases ecstatic. The poems reveal a man of quiet courage, tenderness, sympathy, and humanity. He is the apostle of 'sweetness and light' in its finest sense, yet recognizes with Mr Santayana that 'an inexperienced mind remains a thin mind, no matter how much its vapour may be heated and blown about by the natural passion.' The poems reflect the tendencies and thoughts of his age not only in their images but in their greater freedom of form. Mr Binyon will take his place in the tradition of English poetry. Just where that place will eventually be must be left to the siftings of time 'who choosest all in the end well.'

Mr Binyon is as acutely aware of the barrenness of present day life as Mr Eliot. But he sees that there is also richness and sets the ideal towards which we are to strive. In his 'Alas! what dungeon walls we rear' he warns us of the pass to which we have come; realizing which,

Then we shall feel what we have made
Of one another, and be afraid.

('Auguries IV')

He chooses, however, to dwell on the remedy for such spiritual
dryness. In two short lyrics, 'Song,' 'Nothing is Enough,' he
points the way we must go.

For Mercy, Courage, Kindness, Mirth
There is no measure upon earth;
Nay, they wither, root and stem,
If an end be set to them.
Overbrim and overflow
If your own heart you would know.
For the spirit, born to bless,
Lives but in its own excess.
Nothing is enough!
No, though our all be spent—
Heart's extremest love,
Spirit's whole intent,
All that nerve can feel,
All that brain invent,—
Still beyond appeal
Will divine Desire
Yet more excellent
Precious cost require
Never be content
Of this mortal stuff,—
Till ourselves be fire.
Nothing is enough!

D. H. LAWRENCE: POET

'A Note on His Political Ideology'

I

D. H. LAWRENCE as a man and as a literary figure has been the centre of one of the bitterest controversies in modern literature. He has suffered not only from the misunderstanding of his detractors, but from a faulty emphasis by his disciples. But the injustices will wear themselves out with time and the good will remain. In fact, if the motivation of much of the contemporary poetry is to be understood, the good must remain. Particularly is this true of *Last Poems*, the volume reflecting more clearly than his other volumes the political ideology underlying his work, the subject of the present essay.

We hear much to-day of the revolutionary aspects in the works of the younger poets, among whom Auden, Spender, Day Lewis and MacNeice are the most articulate. The aim of this group is to effect a change in order that life itself will have a chance. We might almost say that their aim is to do for the masses what the Italian renaissance did for the bourgeoisie and aristocracy: free the individual. Lawrence is a pioneer in this post-war renaissance. In poem after poem, particularly in *Last Poems,* he develops his thesis of political freedom: not a political freedom in the narrow meaning of parties, but from the point of view of man's relation to society. Beginning with poems general in their nature, he finally hammers at specific abuses which must be obliterated before the free life is possible. It is strange that those persons who would find in Lawrence a powerful ally are most vocal in their condemnation, simply because of his frankness in the presentation of the offs and ons of sex. Under no circumstances, they would seem to say, must the God-man ever admit to the possession of feet of clay, however thoroughly that clay has been transmuted by the fire of experience into a product unrecognizable from its origins.

Lawrence, a true mystic, dislikes the dialectical processes of the rationalist or the philosopher; but he likes thought. Thought for him is a 'welling up of the unknown life into consciousness,' 'the testing of statements on the touchstone of the conscience,' 'gazing on to the face of life,' 'pondering over experience.' He postulates his castigation of the evils of society on the rejection of the abstract as the sole reality ('Demiurge'), and on the mystical conception expressed in 'The Breath of Life' that if one is to get the zest from life he must face the 'sharp winds of change mingled with the breath of destruction'; on the other hand, if one desires 'to breathe deep sumptuous life, he must breathe all alone, in silence, in the dark, and see nothing.' He amplifies this conception in 'Anaxagoras' and 'Kissing and Horrid Strife' which defines life as being

> for delight, and for bliss
> and dread, and the dark, rolling ominousness of doom
> then the bright dawning of delight again
> from off the sheer white snow, or the poised moon.
>
> ('Anaxagoras')

Facile readers misinterpret the words 'kissing,' 'delight,' 'bliss,' 'dread,' etc. They do not invest them with a sub-surface significance. Now Lawrence does not use terms carelessly. If he uses familiar terms in an esoteric sense, he defines them. If we misunderstand him it is apt to be because we permit the intrusion of what Richards would call a mnemonic irrelevance. Take, for example, the word 'evil' as he uses it. It connotes more to him than to the average person. What he really means, he makes clear in innumerable poems. Evil is that which prevents man from taking his place as a part of creation. Evil is the complete absorption of man in himself so that he is 'absolved

from the sun and the earth and the moon, . . . absolved from
strife and kisses . . . absolved from the meddling of creation,
. . . absolved from the great necessities of being.' It is, moreover, the absorption of man in himself for his own ends
('Strife'), without communion with his fellows ('Murder'). It
is to remain static, to let the soul stagnate from inactivity. Life
is a constant wandering, although not necessarily with a
known goal; and the evil of contemporary civilization lies in
man's cessation from wandering and in his Ixion-like endless
revolution about a fixed point, his own ego. The men, for
example, who sit day after day at the machines are only ani-
mated wheels with fettered souls. They

> Sit in the grey mist of movement which moves not
> and going which goes not
> and doing which does not:
> and being which is not:
> that is, they sit and are evil, in evil,
> grey evil, which has no path, and shows neither light nor dark
> and has no home, no home anywhere.
>
> ('Evil is Homeless')

The evil of contemporary life is, moreover, the 'sneaking
evasion of the responsibility of our own consciousness' under
the cloak of humility because of the influence of the machines.
Even the sun-tanned bathers on the beach know nothing ('the
vibration of the motor-car' having 'bruised their insensitive
bottoms'). They call their state health; Lawrence calls it
'nullity'; because 'only here and there a pair of eyes, haunted,
looks out as if asking; where then is life?' (See also 'The Gods!
The Gods!'). How complete this state of nullity is he expounds
in 'Dark Satanic Mills.' 'Oh, Jesus,' asks Lawrence, 'didn't you
see, when you talked to science this would be the result!'

> And now, the iron has entered into the soul
> and the machine has entangled the brain, and got it fast,

and steel has twisted the loins of man, electricity has
    exploded the heart
and out of the lips of people just strange mechanical
    noises in place of speech.

What is man, that thou art no longer mindful of him!
and the son of man, that thou pitiest him not?
Are these no longer men, these millions, millions?
What are they then?

Lawrence does not stop, however, with generalizations. He decries the machine age because of the change it has effected in men:

    whereas faces now are only human grimaces,
    with eyes like the interiors of stuffy rooms, furnished.

In other words, it has dried up the soul, and has created class distinction ('Masses and Classes'). The faults of contemporary society arise from the evil world-soul, the result of the preponderant number of evil-souls, of men absorbed in their own egos. Financiers, scientists, educators, politicians, and a host of others have not possessed the vision to see themselves in their relation to the world as a whole; which, of course, they must do if the world is to be saved. The world will be saved, says Lawrence, not by a democracy of idea or ideal, nor of property, but by a 'democracy of men, a democracy of touch'; not by 'universalism and cosmopolitanism,' but by the recoil into 'separateness.' That this change is already in the air can be seen, he adds, by observing in every country the young men under thirty.

What does he mean by 'touch?' In a series of epigrams— 'Unhappy Souls,' 'Full Life,' 'People who Care,' 'Non-Existence'—he tells us. It is a mystical state in which man is aware of more than he can ever know. Or, as he expresses it in 'God and the Holy Ghost':

The Holy Ghost is the deepest part of our own consciousness
wherein we know ourself for what we are
and know our dependence on the creative beyond.

So if we go counter to our own deepest consciousness
naturally we destroy the most essential self in us,
and once done, there is no remedy, no salvation for this,
nonentity is our portion.

No one can doubt the sincerity of Lawrence's concern over
the state of the masses. In 'What Have They Done to You?'
'What Is a Man to Do?' and 'City Life' his soul cries out against
the spoliation of man's spirit by the machines and the industrialists, and he regrets his inability to

take the iron hook out their faces, that makes them so drawn,
nor cut the invisible wires of steel that pull them
back and forth, to work,
back and forth to work,
like fearful and corpse-like fishes hooked and being played
by some malignant fisherman on an unseen shore
where he does not choose to land them yet, hooked fishes
          of the factory world.

He is indignant, too, because so few have

          the courage of rosiness in a cabbage world
          fragrance of roses in a stale stink of lies
          rose-leaves to bewilder the clever fools
          and rose-briars to strangle the machine.

Mankind is divided in two ways: vertically, between the
sexes, and horizontally, between the base and beautiful. The
base ones are the small ones, ego-bound, and running in an
enclosed circle of self. Without an ideal toward which to strive,
without a vision beyond themselves, they are lost and become
robots. These robots are, unfortunately, as he has elsewhere
suggested, not only confined to factory and industrial workers;

but, to-day, they are the rulers and the industrialists, themselves rulers of millions of robots of the same fundamental nature. Between the robot-classes and the robot-masses lie the 'last living human beings being ground exceeding small' who must save themselves while the robots destroy themselves, as they surely will ('Give Us the Thebaid'). To those who are alive life means too much to warrant their making revolutions.

'But how,' he asks, are the 'men of the wind and rain, men of the fire and rod . . . going to come forth from the robot mass of rich and poor, mechanical ego-bound myriads?' He says, 'Life will find a way.' The manner in which life will find a way is hinted at in 'Impulse.' Once disillusion falls on living men and they realize that nothing can be done for these 'grey rat-hordes of classes and masses,' they must make the great choice of saving themselves. At that moment the destruction of robots begins, because only the kindness of living women and men has kept them sane. The robot, incapable of love or worship, can only hate; and from this hate will spring the revolution.

In 'Fellow Men,' 'The Sight of God,' 'Souls to Save,' 'When Most Men Die,' 'Love Thy Neighbour' and 'Two Ways of Living and Dying' Lawrence repudiates these robot masses as his fellow-men, because most of them, lacking souls, do not matter in the sight of God. They are machines, which, once they die, cannot be mended. Although man once invented machines, these robot masses are the things the machines themselves have invented. To borrow another figure, humanity needs pruning badly because of the danger of the rotten branches to the parts of the tree that are whole, those parts which we might say are made up of the robot-masses and robot-classes ('Humanity Needs Pruning').

The inferiority of man to the machine he tends ('O Wonderful Machine'), the inability of man to see the beauties of the natural world ('Lonely, Lonesome, Loney—O!' 'Trees in the Garden'), and the poet's ironic implication of man's inability to control Nature ('Storm in the Black Forest') intensify the barrenness of the lives of the robot classes and masses. Or, as he says in 'Classes,' there are two classes of *men:* the very few that look directly into the eyes of God, and a few others who look into the eyes of these other men to see the image of God reflected there. The robots, however—those who deny the gleam—are a 'vast third homogeneous amorphous class of anarchy.'

Lawrence believes that the term 'democracy' is generally misunderstood. Democracy is service, but it is not to serve the common people. Democracy is the service of the common people to life. In other words, the masses best serve life as they are able to catch the gleam from the face of the few who look directly upon God ('Democracy is Service'). This is not as vague as it might at first appear. As he elaborates the idea in 'False Democracy and Real,' man without an ideal toward which to strive, without a vision beyond himself, is lost and becomes a robot. 'Service' develops Lawrence's thesis:

> Ah yes, men must learn to serve
> not for money, but for life.

> Ah yes, men must learn to obey
> not a boss, but the gleam of life on the face of a man
> who has looked into the eyes of the gods.

> Man is only perfectly human
> when he looks beyond humanity.

Lawrence decries the harmful attitude of the sentimentalist toward the social problem. Man must have the courage and ability for clarity of vision. Man is not helped by blinding himself to reality; but by recognizing it and fighting against it ('Retort to Whitman'). Unlike the result of a running contest, the race of life is not to the swift, but to the person who can so efface himself that his soul is not trampled in the mud ('Race and Battle').

Lawrence elsewhere voices his concern over the precarious position of the valuers of life. Between the bourgeois and the bolshevist with their conflicting ideas of property we shall all be cut to bits ('Property and No-Property'). The reader will see that Day Lewis, Auden, and Spender express this same view. As Lawrence sees it, but one solution presents itself. Man will become interested in something else to the extent that the property problem solves itself ('The Way Out'); or, more explicitly, man will interest himself in nature and in man to the extent that nothing else will matter ('If You Are a Man').

> To know the moon as we have never known
> yet she is knowable
> To know a man as we have never known
> a man, as never yet a man was knowable, yet still shall be.

The beauty of an instant realized is in strong contrast to the ironic poems 'Broadcasting to the G.B.P.' and 'We Can't Be Too Careful,' in which the public is looked upon as little more than probing infants, and incapable of thought.

None of Lawrence's poems clinches the effectiveness of his forceful appeal for the full life more than do the later poems on death; none is more moving and beautiful. To the man who has lived there is a gladness unlike that of the slave of the machines ('Gladness of Death'). Death is a release from the place where

> Men prevent one another from being men
> but in the great spaces of death
> the winds of the afterwards kiss us into
> blossom of manhood.

To accomplish the full life does not imply the necessity of self-sacrifice. As Lawrence says, 'It cannot be anything but wrong to sacrifice good, healthy, natural feelings, instincts, passions or desires.' All that we may sacrifice 'are all the obstructions to life, self-importance, self-conceit, egoistic self-will, or all the ugly old possessions that make up the impediments of life. . . .' ('Self-Sacrifice.')

What he desires for men is summed up in 'Flowers and Men':

> All I want of you, men and women,
> all I want of you
> is that you shall achieve your beauty
> as the flowers do.

Seen from this point of vantage how different an interpretation of the poems in *Collected Poems* is not only possible, but necessary. In order to shock the reader into an awareness of self and of his position in life he has many times over-stressed his thesis with the result that the facile reader has misinterpreted him. From a few isolated examples he has made faulty generalizations; and has arrived at erroneous conclusions.

I think Lawrence's aim is expressed in 'Vibration of Justice' and 'The Deepest Sensuality.' He realizes with Santayana that there can be no knowledge without emotion. He wishes to stir us to the point when

> The profound and thrilling vibrations of justice, sense of ultimate justice
> makes the heart suddenly quiver with love.

In the present exposition of Lawrence's political ideas the word 'god' has frequently appeared. What is Lawrence's concept of the term? Creative work, he says, is not the product of thought but of a great urge within us that cannot foresee the product ('The Work of Creation'). God, he adds in 'The Body of God,' 'is the great urge that has not yet found a body, but urges towards incarnation with the great creative urge':

> There is no god
> apart from poppies, and the flying fish,
> men singing songs, and women brushing their hair in the sun.
> The lovely things are god that has come to pass, like Jesus came,
> The rest, the undiscoverable, is the demiurge.

God, like the rainbow, is something on which you cannot lay your hand . . . nor even your mind. 'There Are No Gods' is an even better exposition of his belief. Lawrence is, like the early Wordsworth, a pantheist. A look into a great full lime-tree of summer was for him a vision 'deep into the eyes of gods' ('What Are the Gods?').

In the light of the foregoing not only can the spiritual quality of 'God and the Holy Ghost,' 'The Gods! The Gods!' and 'Name the Gods!' not be denied, but it must stand out as the flowering of a great and magnanimous soul. What Lawrence wishes to stress, I think, is the idea that we are only capable of seeing truth when our emotions are in play. Lawrence is a true mystic in the literal meaning of the term.

II

But what of the clothing in which he has dressed his ideas? To-day when the new poetry is difficult to read, the clarity of Lawrence's expression is apt to mislead the reader into placing too low a value on his poetic achievement. *Last Poems* is not the finished product that *Collected Poems* is—it was published posthumously and not prepared for the press by Lawrence— but every selection reveals ample evidences of real poetry. The images are fresh, forceful, and accurate; the language is salty, pungent, and at times acrid.

The form of the poems in *Last Poems* is freer than that in *Collected Poems*, marking an advance beyond the already free structure of *Birds, Beasts and Flowers*. In fact many of them could fittingly be called prose poems. By this greater freedom of form Lawrence is able to achieve a fullness that otherwise would be impossible. 'Lord's Prayer,' for example, is dithyrambic in quality.

He uses repetition effectively. In 'Stoic' the word 'groan' directs and controls the reader's emotional reaction to the idea, particularly its use in the last ten verses. So, too, does the incremental use of 'bigger' in the satiric 'We Can't Be Too Careful.' The idea that there are other ways of reaching God than through the Christian religion, ways which are more suggestive, more pliant, less hard is onomatopoetically suggested in 'Bells.'

Lawrence's language is always strongly metaphorical, as the foregoing selections amply testify. Nature invariably moves him to a quickened activity in the creation of images. The figure of the sun 'like a lion' and the moon 'like a queen' in 'The Argonants' is but one example:

Now that the sun, like a lion, licks his paws
and goes slowly down the hill:
now that the moon, who remembers, and only cares
that we should be lovely in the flesh, with bright, crescent feet,
pauses near the crest of the hill, climbing slowly, like a queen
looking down on the lion as he retreats.

The language of 'The Ship of Death' is an even better illustration.

But this is not the place for a detailed discussion of Lawrence's prosody. A just estimate is possible only from an analysis of the rhyming as well as of the unrhyming poems. Such a study in an essay primarily concerned with the interpretation of one phase of his work, his political ideology, would be comparable to the tail of a St Bernard attached to the body of a mouse: the body would not only be wagged but would be almost totally obscured.

There is too great a tendency to look upon the poems in *Last Poems* as fragmentary. This is unfortunate, because a true estimate of them can only be had by looking upon them as epigrams in the Greek sense of the term: short poems embodying a mood or idea of the author.

The reaction to Lawrence's poems is largely determined, I think, by the time point of view of the reader. If he looks forward to them from a position conditioned by nineteenth century standards he will see them as a chaotic defiance of tradition in thought, morality, and pattern. If he looks back upon them from a position conditioned by the standards of the most recent poetry he will see them as a rich fecundating loam. Neither view is correct. They are capable of standing by themselves as the last expression of a man of comprehensive soul little understood by either his admirers or his detractors.

THE POETRY OF T. S. ELIOT

THE recent publication of *The Family Reunion*, Mr T. S. Eliot's latest essay in dramatic form, will partially resolve a problem that has long confronted many of his readers, that of the reconciliation of a qualified admiration for the clothing of the ideas with an intellectual and emotional disagreement with the ideas themselves. It cannot be wholly resolved until a later work affirms and carries forward his belatedly discovered conviction. The present acceptance of his work depends upon a state of willing suspension of disagreement on the part of the reader, which, however, is difficult to prolong after laying aside the poetry. A criticism of the basic ideas so obviously the result of an intensely personal reaction to life must also be personal and will be conditioned by the thought and experience of the critic. It is therefore advisable, I think, before considering the aesthetic problem first to attempt a valuation of the poet's ideas.

For some time I have believed that Mr Eliot was the victim of an unfortunate education. His mentors, like those of John Stuart Mill, concentrated on the development of his intellect and neglected that larger subject without which intellect can be but a negative force—humanity. Only lately has he seen the necessity for schooling himself in this field. The turning point is visible in 'Ash Wednesday,' but it does not actually occur until after 'Journey of the Magi,' 'A Song for Simeon,' and 'Animula,' and is not fully effected even in *The Family Reunion*.

The generations of young men of precious childhood and education who, because of a belated contact with reality, suffer disillusionment when brought into contact with the commonness of the average man of the street, will find in the early poetry an accurate reflection of their reactions. To those, however, who because of earlier associations suffer no disillusionment, although regretting that reality is not different, and to the more courageous mature persons who have gained tolerance and understanding from an experience which cuts vertically through life, the early poetry will be valuable for the search after and frequent success in finding new rhythms and new images for a fresh and effective communication.

Mr Eliot's one-man show contains caricatures, line drawings, modern imitations of Hogarth, and abstract self-portraits of his soul. J. Alfred Prufrock, for example, has reality only in the mind of Mr Eliot. He is an interesting caricature, but only that. We can admire the technique, the freshness of approach, the vivid touches of colour, but we must not mistake it for a likeness of Mr Prufrock. The portrait is as a younger man would understand him. It possesses Mr Eliot's great defect—a defect as evident in his late as in his early poetry—his inability to enter into the mind of his subject or to comprehend a soul-state other than his own. It is not that he lacks sympathy, but he does not realize where sympathy is necessary. The background against which Prufrock moves is falsified by over-simplification. The same criticism is applicable to 'Portrait of a Lady.' The lady is an obvious distortion; the painter fills the foreground of the canvas with a large self-portrait.

The same criticism is valid of Mr Eliot's pictures of lower class society. In the third of the 'Preludes,' for example, he endows the house-maid with certain mental awarenesses that she probably never experienced, and deprives her of any qualities of 'soul-state.' The poet's uneasy apprehension that he had not seen to the hearts of his characters is suggested in the fourth prelude:

> I am moved by fancies that are curled
> Around these images, and cling;
> The notion of some infinitely gentle
> Infinitely suffering thing.

Unfortunately, however, he continued to paint as he had been painting, sacrificing truth for cleverness. Mrs Phlaccus, Professor and Mrs Cheetah, the characters in 'The Boston Evening Transcript,' Sweeney and his associates swell the gallery. Sweeney, for example, is a composite portrait of vulgarized lower-class society from which the painter has been careful to filter every trace that might lighten the effect. It is a forceful portrait, but it has no depth, no counterpart in life.

In these early poems Mr Eliot presents the facts and leaves the reader to discover the moral. His outraged idealism has engendered bitterness. He fails to see that the trouble lies in an idealism built on illusion rather than reality. 'Gerontion' expresses his conviction that the world is a waste land. Seeing that from whatever class of society Mr Eliot draws his subjects he finds only characters like Bleistein, Princess Volupine, and Sir Ferdinand Klein with Mr Silvero, Madame de Tornquist, Hakagawa, and Fraulein von Kulp filling in the background (the names themselves suggest a universal application), it is little wonder that his attempt at a more ambitious work results in 'The Waste Land.' On his larger canvas he again simplifies—this time those things which he had already oversimplified.

The error arises from his belief that he cuts life vertically, whereas he has only a horizontal knowledge of life: that is, he knows but one class of society, and views all others from that point of vision. He is a snob without being aware of it. The tragedy lies in his conviction that he has given a realistic portrayal—one, in fact, that brought him to the edge of despair—and the rejection of his portrayal as untrue to facts by all save those whose limited experience makes them incapable of judging. The artist has failed in his attempt to communicate a universal message. One admires the unified tone, the technical craftsmanship, the subtle variation within a narrow range, the truth of many details, but he turns with relief to canvases possessing a greater fidelity to nature when a synthesis on a larger scale has been effected.

Mr Eliot frequently looks to the early seventeenth century as a period when he would have been happy. We need only remember the intense disillusionment of the youthful Milton at corrupt conditions and lack of nobility during this very period that stands out as a beacon for Mr Eliot, to be reminded that every idealist lays too great a stress on those qualities which becloud his ideal.

Milton differed markedly, of course, from Mr Eliot; and in that difference probably lies the reason for the latter's lack of appreciation of him. Milton did not withdraw into himself and attempt to avoid reality. He did not retard his development by trying to escape. He struck out boldly. He feared no chimeras and he fought to make his idealism a reality in the world. He possesses a largeness of soul that is an excellent corrective to the diseased introspection of many contemporary writers. Those who disagree with Mr Eliot's point of view do not take the silly optimistic view of Pangloss that everything is for the best in this best of all regulated worlds; but they do see qualities in the subjects chosen by Mr Eliot that he does not see—or is only now beginning to see. They feel a great share of the waste land lies within himself.

'The Waste Land' remains for many an incomprehensible poem. I shall later point out what I feel to be its defects as well as its merits. But the basic ideas are clearly stated. The world is a waste land in which no one can have a realization of the significance of life unless he can make a synthesis of his experiences. 'A heap of broken images'—and I agree with the poet's statement in 'The Burial of the Dead'—is the sum total of most lives. That the condition is not endemic to one class only is the statement of 'A Game of Chess;' just as 'The Fire Sermon' contrasts the barrenness of the present with the richness of the past. By such over-simplification Mr Eliot obviously is a party to a falsification which at the time of writing was, of course, an unconscious falsification. He overlooked the fact that in retrospect it is chiefly the spiritual monuments that remain. (We have only to think of Ozymandias.) 'Death by Water' warns us that death comes to all; and since we cannot escape it we should live to be ready for it. After surveying the contemporary ruin of civilization and seeing no hope—of the human duty, give; of the angelic duty, sympathize; of the godly duty, control—Mr Eliot decides to look out for himself—to set his own lands in order. This section—'What the Thunder Said'—contains the most moving poetry to be found in the whole corpus of Mr Eliot's work. In the passage 'Here is no water but only rock' beginning with a symbolic picture of the contemporary scene, the poet forces us into that willing suspension of disagreement of which I have spoken, and drags us with him to the depths of despair. 'The Hollow Men,' keyed in the same mood as 'The Waste Land,' is a desolate picture of men devoid of spiritual natures; men completely empty. Man going against his inner nature by paying homage only to material things loses his soul:

> At the hour when we are
> Trembling with tenderness
> Lips that would kiss
> Form prayers to broken stone

Section IV more than hints at Mr Eliot's slowly forming opinion that the only hope lies in religion. Life disappointed Mr Eliot just as, for a time, it later disappointed Mr Spender. It proved to be no antagonist who once engaged in open combat and decisively defeated, would then remain permanently subdued. It was 'the gradual day weakening the will' and ending 'not with a bang but a whimper' that baffled them.

With 'The Hollow Men' Mr Eliot's first poetic phase draws to a close, a phase which has exerted an as yet incalculable force on the direction taken by our younger poets. Yet it is a force that for natural reasons seems to be losing its potency. Mr Eliot's problem has been a personal one—that of an expatriate. He shut himself off from the restorative powers provided by

an America transforming itself and was denied the early
influence of the English countryside so important in moulding
the English youth. He sees nature only in its cruellest aspects—
the struggle for the survival of the stronger. But few persons,
I believe, think of this aspect when drinking in the May-morn-
ing spirit of the English countryside.

The early phase actually closes, however, with 'Journey of
the Magi' and 'A Song for Simeon,' poems indicating the direction the new phase must take. They are easier, less forceful, and
resigned. No longer does the poet look upon his age as peculiar in its barrenness; every age has been so. Even at the birth
of Christ a vast part of life was a desert. There never has been
a golden age. But set down this, said the old Magi:

> this Birth was
> Hard and bitter agony for us, like Death, our death.
> We returned to our places, these kingdoms,
> But no longer at ease here, in the old dispensation,
> With an alien people clutching their gods.
> I should be glad of another death.

'A Song for Simeon' is of the same spiritual period as
'Journey of the Magi.' The movement of the verse, strongly
ritualistic in quality, marks a relaxation from the tension of
'The Waste Land,' 'The Hollow Men,' and the poems preceding them. It imparts a sense of relief of being freed from a
heavy burden. The full realization of the catastrophe has
struck Simeon and he is resigned, resigned to his own fate and
to that of his children's children who will 'take to the goat's
path, and the fox's home.'

The lesson that can be deduced from the early poetry—that
the child is father to the man—is substantiated in *Animula*. It is
true of a certain group that

> The heavy burden of the growing soul
> Perplexes and offends more, day by day;
> Week by week, offends and perplexes more

With the imperatives of 'is and seems'
And may and may not, desire and control.
The pain of living and the drug of dreams
Curl up the small soul in the window seat
Behind the *Encyclopedia Britannica*,

and that this group grows into a distorted maturity; but it is
only true of a certain group. There is a middle way between
easy optimism and the hopelessness of despair.

With 'Ash Wednesday,' his greatest poetic achievement, Mr
Eliot enters his second poetic phase. The poem, opening on a
note of lost idealism, continues the thought that the world is a
waste land. The most the poet can hope for in the air 'which is
now thoroughly small and dry' is to learn 'to care and not to
care,' to learn how 'to sit still.' The world in which the inhabitants have not yet made a synthesis of their lives will not heed
the cries of warning. They continue their disjointed, barren
lives. The poet, seeking to save himself by turning to religion
and determined to put his own house in order, found a
'strength beyond hope and despair' as he climbed ever higher.
Formalized religion does not rest easily on Mr Eliot's shoul-
ders. There is too great a sense of effort in his determination to
find salvation from that source. Instead of convincing the
reader that he has found it, he only convinces him that he has
made a great intellectual effort to believe and that his faith does
not well from within. The humility is not a genuine humility,
and the reader senses it. The poem ends, as it began, on a note
of despair.

'Sweeney Agonistes,' 'Triumphal March,' and *The Rock* add
little to what the poet has already said, except by way of
emphasis. How Mr Eliot hates the common people! One
regrets that he did not grow up in a small town where he could
not have escaped knowing some of them. He would then have
had more tolerance, although his poetry might have had less
force. His poetic strength frequently lies in the concentration

of a narrow vision. *The Rock*, for which Mr Eliot disclaims any responsibility except for the words, is one of the most flagrant displays of over-weening arrogance on the part of the clerics that I have ever angered through, in spite of a frequent high quality in the poetry that displays Mr Eliot's remarkable ability in the handling of rhythms to communicate dignity, despair, and irony.

Murder in the Cathedral marks a change in Mr Eliot's attitude that becomes more sharply pronounced in *The Family Reunion*. In this dramatic essay Mr Eliot combines and rounds out the various phases through which he has passed and makes possible a synthesis of his work from the early Prufrock to his latest opus. The theme is the impossibility of happiness or satisfaction to one who attempts to evade the responsibilities of life. Only by facing the problem squarely can one avoid a delayed emotional maturity. The play echoes and re-echoes ideas from the earlier work, but carries those ideas to their conclusion. Harry, the protagonist, realizes the barrenness of the life about him, realizes that the ordinary day of many is not much more than breathing, that life to a vast number is but an impact of external events, that it is without reason, without direction, without purpose, that too many have lost their way in the dark. Man is not free but depends too much on the opinion of his neighbours; he is neither sure of himself nor of the world he lives in. If he is to find happiness, however, he cannot get out of the swell of the sea and try to save himself by evasion. He must move forward courageously even though the struggle is painful and dangerous. The key of this new note is found in Agatha's speech to Harry:

> Whatever you have learned, Harry, you must remember
> That there is always more: we cannot rest in being
> The impatient spectators of malice or stupidity.
> We must try to penetrate the other private worlds
> Of make-believe and fear. To rest in our own suffering
> Is evasion of suffering. We must learn to suffer more.

In other speeches she stresses the fact that what Harry must do is not for everyone; only for those with the inner desire. Each must fight his own battle. Says Agatha:

Success is relative:
It is what we can make of the mess we have made of things,
It is what he can make, not what you would make for him.

* * * * *

For those who live in this world, this world only,
Do you think that I would take the responsibility
Of tempting them over the border? No one could, no one who knows.

The spirit of this new note is similar to that of 'George Gray' in *The Spoon River Anthology*.

Although the change in tone is a welcome change, there is something sad about it, too. It has taken Mr Eliot fifty years to find out what many dimly perceive at twenty and so choose a way of life, which brings satisfaction at thirty, and from which they begin to reap an abundant harvest at forty. What has been the effect on his poetry of the growing sense of a necessity for a greater humanity? Although the reader need no longer put himself in a willing suspension of disagreement, I am afraid that the change in the poetry itself conveys the impression of a relaxation. A tardy realization of the problem of life has been accompanied by a lack of force in the rhythms.

II

The problem of the clothing of the foregoing ideas—more important, I think, than the ideas themselves—has already been treated in detail by numerous critics. With much that has been said I heartily concur; with much else I dissent. 'The Love Song of J. Alfred Prufrock' is a remarkable *tour de force* in rhythm and imagery. Youthful effort, a conscious straining for effect—is everywhere visible, particularly in several of the images. The much discussed description of the evening 'spread out against the sky like a patient etherized upon the table' has always struck me as a poor one because vague. To one person it is a cold aquamarine sky, to another it is a sky streaked with red, to a third it is a soft delicately flushed sky. The latter more nearly resembles an etherized patient. Much cleverer is the description of the fog as an animal, in spite of the sense of effort which it communicates to the reader. On the other hand, the oft-repeated refrain

> In the room the women come and go
> Talking of Michelangelo

and the typical Eliotian 'I have measured out my life in coffee spoons' are excellent crystallizations of mood and character. The qualities brought to a greater degree of effectiveness in the later work—wit, humour, incisiveness, intricate rhythmical patterns, an exquisite ear—are, in fact, all found in this early work. In 'Portrait of a Lady' the situation is even more vividly conceived and the person who has had an experience similar to that of the poet is highly amused; particularly at the appropriateness of 'My smile falls heavily among the bric-a-brac.' The studiedly unromantic epithets of the moon in 'Rhapsody on a Windy Night' accord well with the tone of the poem. Donne-like in quality is the description of the street 'held in a lunar synthesis.' The characteristic feature of these early poems is a vivid, photographic eye intimately bound up with seventeenth century wit. In particular instances, however, Mr Eliot's attempts at fixing characters 'in a formulated phrase' lead him into gross mis-statements. When he speaks, for example, of housemaids 'sprouting despondently at area gates' he both succeeds and fails. 'Despondently' is as unfortunate as 'sprouting' is happy. And in telling us that Mr Appolinax laughed like an 'irresponsible foetus,' what does he mean?

Mr Eliot makes a sparing use of simile. In *Poems: 1909–1925*, for example, there are scarcely a dozen, none of them drawn from nature. His use of metaphor, however, is the reverse. Nothing is said in unfigurative language if a metaphor could possibly be used. This use of metaphor, although accounting for the highly charged quality of his verse, is also responsible for the accompanying sense of effort and self-consciousness. Mr Eliot is never spontaneous; he never succeeds in making us forget the labour spent. His is not an art that conceals art.

With greater maturity the early exaggerations tend to disappear. In 'Gerontion' the rhythms become more subtle, the conviction more passionate, with a correspondingly more effective communication of a sense of futility. A more obvious communication of this sense of disillusionment is found in those poems in which he employs a quatrain whose movement is the very apotheosis of dryness. The music of 'Burbank with a Baedecker: Bleistein with a Cigar,' 'The Cooking Egg,' the Sweeney poems, and 'The Hippopotamus' communicates a sense of ignorance, materialism, vulgarity, and grossness of the world that appals one—that would overpower him did he believe the picture more than a surface impression.

In 'The Waste Land' a new problem confronts the reader: the problem that many will not take the trouble to solve, or, if the trouble is taken, do not feel the effort worthwhile, namely the problem of esoteric allusion. On the whole I do not think the poem gains much richness in communication even if one takes the trouble to track down the allusions. For a passage to be effective in evoking associational overtones it must be one that is not buried too deeply in the subconscious mind. They should be allusions that are part of the heritage of one well-versed, or even fairly well-versed, in the major literary monuments of the past—not merely those esoteric works which have made an impress on the mind of the poet. When Mr Eliot, for example, uses allusions based on Miss Jessie Weston's *From Ritual to Romance*, he gains little and loses much. It is a conscious transference, and being such is imperfectly assimilated. After reading *From Ritual to Romance* I do not think Mr

Eliot's use of the material repaid the effort from the point of view of a greater appreciation of 'The Waste Land.' The book, however, is thoroughly enjoyable. In 'The Game of Chess,' too, my reaction was the same. I had already read *The Change-ling* before turning seriously to 'The Waste Land.' My subconscious memory was not stirred. And when I re-read the play, I still thought Mr Eliot's associational use of one episode extremely esoteric. So it is with many of the other allusions in the poem. When, however, he draws from what is more common in our heritage, his assimilation of the material conveys a sense of greater completeness, and we find an enhanced richness of overtone. The echoes from Shakespeare, Spenser, and Wagner—to name the more effective ones—arouse in us a more heightened enjoyment of the passage than would otherwise be possible. A later age, more familiar with much of this material, might possibly derive from the poem overtones which to most of the present age are impossible.

On the other hand the poet attains new heights in the subtlety of his rhythms. An outstanding example is a passage to which I have already referred. It begins slowly and sadly 'Here is no water but only rock,' gathers momentum to the line 'Dead mountain mouth of carious teeth that cannot spit,' subsides slowly, and ends in an anguish of despair that wrings one's heart:

If there were water

    And no rock
    If there were rock
    And also water
    And water
    A spring
    A pool among the rock
    If there were the sound of water only
    Not the cicada
    And dry grass singing
    But sound of water over a rock

> Where the hermit-thrush sings in the pine trees
> Drip drop drip drop drop drop drop
> But there is no water

'The Hollow Men' is similarly effective, particularly the falling off of the ending.

The rhythms of 'Journey of the Magi,' 'Song for Simeon,' and 'Animula' mark a distinct relaxation from those of the early work. They indicate a fatigue which well accords with their subject matter. The images, too, are simplified; they are wholly traditional.

'Ash Wednesday,' however, marks for me Mr Eliot's most successful poetic achievement. No awkward joining is visible in the relation of the parts. It has a greater architectonic unity than any major poem he has written before or since; it has the quality of a Bach fugue. The manner, for example, in which 'Teach us to care and not to care/Teach us to sit still' is woven into the first and last sections, is but one instance. Nowhere is Mr Eliot so completely the poet, the poet of decorative elegance of the Tennysonian school. Repeated readings of the poem enhance its stature. The manner in which he weaves and interweaves delicately curving, smoothly flowing lines—always consciously, of course—is Gothic in feeling. As he escapes 'the deceitful face of hope and of despair still visible from the third stair,' the rhythms become less dry, more gracious, culminating in the passage:

> Blown hair is sweet, brown hair over the mouth blown,
> Lilac and brown hair;
> Distraction, music of the flute, stops and steps of
>   the mind over the third stair.
> Fading, fading; strength beyond hope and despair
> Climbing the third stair.

Even more subtle is the interweaving of 'word' and 'world' and the single 'whirled,' carrying with it a further association from the use of the words in 'Gerontion.'

Since 'Ash Wednesday' Mr Eliot's poetry has changed
noticeably. 'Triumphal March' is interesting in the contrast of
the eager movement of the first part—the rabble's curiosity—
with that section depicting the hero, the epitome of self-
control:

> There is no interrogation in those eyes
> Or in the hands, quiet over the horse's neck,
> And the eyes watchful, waiting, perceiving, indifferent . . .

More important, however, is the gradual extension of the
emotional range resulting from the poet's changing concept of
his relation to man. *The Rock*, as I have mentioned, contains
poetic passages of a calibre which reveal the poet's remarkable
ability in the handling of rhythms to communicate dignity,
despair, and irony.

This extension of range is even more noticeable in *Murder in
the Cathedral*. In the final analysis, I think the value of this
dramatic essay will lie in its poetry rather than its drama. In
spite of superficial resemblances to the Greek drama—the use
of stichomythy and the inability of the chorus to act being but
two—it has little or none of its inner quality. I felt the essential
undramatic quality of the play at the first reading, experienced
the same reaction at the London performance, and have been
confirmed in that reaction by subsequent readings. The appeal
lies in the choruses of the women of Canterbury and the
speeches of Becket regarded as poetry rather than drama. The
characters are wooden and imperfectly defined. Even the
conception of Becket is confused. Mr Eliot, here as elsewhere,
is incapable of entering the minds of his characters. They remain, therefore, the means by which he develops his meta-
physics. When he succeeds in investing the exposition of his
ideas with passion the play comes to life. As an evening of
poetry reading the play is beautiful; as drama it is a failure.

I spoke of Mr Eliot's ability in 'Ash Wednesday' to weave a
delicate tracery of ornament by repetition of word and phrase.

In *Murder in the Cathedral* he practices this ability on a more
varied scale. At times it is the repetition of one letter (alliteration), at others the repetition of one word, again a whole
phrase, and in at least one instance an entire paragraph. The
Fourth Tempter's speech (p. 40), for example, is identical with
Thomas' speech (p. 21) except for the substitution of 'you' for
'they.' In production this would necessarily be overlooked.

Frequently, the poet heightens the dramatic effect by a
gradually increasing pace of the rhythms as in the Chorus—
'Here is no continuing city,' until towards the end they pile up.
The strong ritualistic quality of the verse, already evident in
'Ash Wednesday' and 'Song for Simeon,' is particularly
apparent in the chorus 'I have smelt them, the death bringers
. . .' The verse is capable of communicating wheedling, seductive, gentle, and dignified moods, the couplets being particularly effective for sarcasm and hate. In *The Family Reunion* there
is the same use of stichomythia, the same ritualistic movement
of the verse, and the same undramatic quality to the speeches
as in *Murder in the Cathedral*. Mr Eliot shows an increasing
tendency to shed much of the 'decorative elegance' brought to
a high state in 'Ash Wednesday.' Important as the play is in a
study of the development of the poet's philosophy, it adds
little to his poetic stature.

Several critics have spoken of Mr Eliot's imagery, of his
conscious use of sources, and of the influence of the work of
the French symbolists on him. Frequently, however, verbal
echoes from unsuspected sources creep into his work. On two
occasions, for example, he echoes Rupert Brooke. 'They bathe
all day and they dance all night' recalls 'They bathe by day,
they bathe by night' from *The Old Vicarage, Grantchester*, and I
strongly suspect his influence in some of the earlier work.
There, however, it is that of Brooke the idealist who would be
a realist, the Brooke of 'Channel Crossing.' But this is a matter
of little importance. I feel certain that Mr Eliot would like to
overlook it. The most striking characteristic of Mr Eliot's

imagery, as I have already mentioned in connection with his similes, is the almost complete absence of images based on nature. Mr Eliot is always the city-bred poet.

From the foregoing discussion of the thought underlying Mr Eliot's poetry and the clothing of that thought, certain conclusions are obvious. The most glaring fault is the complete lack of humanity that is everywhere visible until its first faint glimmerings in *Murder in the Cathedral* and *The Family Reunion*, a lack arising from the fact that he has attempted to apply his narrow knowledge of life derived from a particular stratum of society to all classes. Without being personal, it is obvious that his father did not share the educational theories of the father of Montaigne. He is ill-equipped by early training and temperament to cut through life vertically. His later work announces with the air of discovery what most persons have long taken for granted. Instead of being startled, they merely mutter that it was about time.

Prosodically, Mr Eliot has made an important contribution in pruning away excrescenses from poetry that had been slowly accumulating among second rate poets. The best poets (at least in their best work) have always been free of them. It is unfortunate that Mr Eliot's critics have not been content to praise him for this achievement without trying to do so at the expense of such poets as Milton, Keats, or Tennyson. What they did has no possible connection with his field. He has worked in the tradition of Donne, Dryden, and the later satirists; they in the more powerful tradition of English poetry. In his narrow field, Mr Eliot has worked carefully and well. In his poetry he is always the poet; in his thinking, he is always Mr Eliot.

HUGH MacDIARMID

WITHIN recent years poetry has again swung decidedly to the left.[1] So marked is this tendency that it is in danger of becoming a literary pose rather than the expression of a passionate conviction. In England, the movement is understandable because of two dominant factors: the first and most important is the sudden awakening of the young intellectual to the conditions of the labouring classes brought about by the general strike of 1926 when, for the first time, he was brought into contact with reality; the second is the impetus to this awakened sensibility given by D. H. Lawrence. In Scotland, too, the movement has found its interpreter in the work of the ardent and impassioned nationalist, Mr Hugh MacDiarmid,[2] who, through the medium of metrical language in Scots dialect and in English, has given expression to his wide range of interests. Mr MacDiarmid is at present, I believe, known but to a comparatively small circle of American readers; and the fault is largely his own that that circle is not wider. The subject matter of his poetry is provocative and substantial, and in his more recent work the expression is straightforward and simple and in an easily understood idiom. But the extreme use of an esoteric dialect in his earlier volumes obscured the essential simplicity of many lyrics and made difficult the apprehension of the philosophic nature of such a work as *Circumjcck Cencrastus*.[3] Compared with his Southern neighbour the Scots

[1] I say 'again' advisedly. Had the late eighteenth and early nineteenth centuries had the same predilection for the word 'left' as we, they certainly would have applied it to the poetry of the day.

[2] Mr C. M. Grieve has progressively spelt his pen name M'Diarmid, McDiarmid, and Mac Diarmid.

[3] The general reader would do well to make his first acquaintance with Mr MacDiarmid through the volume *Second Hymn to Lenin and Other Poems*, and follow it with Mr MacDiarmid's own selection of his earlier poems. He can then fill in the gaps as he becomes more familiar with his mode of communication. The following is a partial bibliography. *Sangschaw* (1915); *Penny Wheep* (1926); *The Lucky Bag* (1927); *A Drunk Man Looks at the Thistle* (1926); *To Circumjack Cencrastus* (1930); *First Hymn to Lenin and Other Poems* (1931); *Scots Unbound* (1932); *Stony Limits and Other Poems* (1934); *Selected Poems* (1934); *Second Hymn to Lenin etc.* (1935).

Lowlander has always been less imaginative and more philosophic. He has exalted the powers of reason. Mr MacDiarmid
is no exception. His poetry not only teems with ideas stimu-
lated by a close knowledge of the British as well as the con-
tinental philosophers, but reveals the poet philosophizing on
his own profession. Too many times, however, he forgets his
duty as a poet and his expression becomes matter-of-fact. He
fails to communicate to the reader the enthusiasm which the
idea probably aroused in him. With his predilection for philosophy, it is not strange, therefore, to find that in his poetry he
has developed at considerable length his conception of the
function of a poet, that he has beaten out his own personal
philosophy, crystallizing the distilled essence of a moment
realized in love or nature, in addition to having presented his
strong convictions on politics, religion, patriotism, and
nationalism.

Differing markedly from the intuitive Lawrence, Mr Mac-
Diarmid likes thought. He likes poems that are dry and hard
—and not those which, suiting the general taste, are 'fozy wi'
infinity.' Thought is attractive to him because it leads to the
only things worth having. It has, moreover, kept him from the
belief that the best way of life is that of him who in the material
processes of life lays waste his powers. As he remarks in 'De
Profundis,' and even more forcefully in 'Folly', the wise man
is the one whom the world frequently takes to be the fool. He
has chosen to *live*, whereas the majority in the world have
spent 'their lives wasting the reasons for living.' Most persons
are apathetic until something stirs them from their lethargy,
even though that something might have to be death ('Salmon
Leap').

Thought has also led him to explore the paradox of genius,
the unexplainable. Extending the basic idea of Shelley's 'Hymn
to Intellectual Beauty,' he expresses the need of a 'technique
for genius,' because as matters now stand we cannot tell from
whence it will spring—certainly good birth is no criterion

('The Burning Passion'). Or, failing that, we need to find a means whereby all that genius has accomplished will be the starting point of all men's lives. The inadequacy of language to communicate a truly mystical experience presents a serious obstacle to such an accomplishment. The mind of man can create no ideas although 'it is ideas alone that create.' Or, expressed more clearly in the final stanza of 'Birth of a Genius Among Men,' he mentions how, while lying awake, he

... heard the faint voices of them discuss
The way in which they could only express themselves yet
In fragmentary and fallacious forms through us,

an idea which bears a startling resemblance to Protagoras' belief that man is the measure of things.

Although he will not pander to the popular taste, Mr Mac-Diarmid has little patience with those poets who do not write for the masses of men or who are content to copy the themes used by their predecessors. Poets cannot produce great work and at the same time surrender to the crowd. If their work is to be worth reading, they must think for themselves, not be content to work over the notions of 'slaverin' savages.' Since ours is 'a frenzied and chaotic age,' it becomes increasingly necessary to find 'men capable of rejecting all that other men think, as a stone remains the essential to the world, inseparable from it.' In regard to themselves, however, Mr MacDiarmid believes that 'maist men are prehistoric still!' In this group he places some of the great Victorians as well as Goethe, who since he did not get beneath the surface of life, has no message for mankind; he lacks universality.

To his statement that the soul has a right to change according to its impacts, impacts which preclude the possibility of a poet's dwelling in an ivory tower, no one will object. Nor will he, however, find anything particularly new in such an idea. How is growth measured but by the changing soul?[1] That

---

[1] 'Soul' is a dangerous word. It, too, is 'fozy wi' infinity'.

poetry no longer holds the exalted place in man's life that it once did, he would be the first to admit. Or, expressed differently, 'Nature never abandoned a fairer aince-mair-promisin' field.' Although poetry as embodied in particular poems does not seem to be permanent—like a life that is lived bravely for a moment and then goes 'away to the void again'—it only seems so because we ourselves are so temporary.

Such are some of his general ideas about poetry. In particular it should be the property of the man in the street; it should concern itself with 'real ends,' i.e., vital problems, because it would then be the world's greatest force for good; it should get to the very essence of the thing; it must be the result of an examination of all phases of life with which the poet has closely associated himself in order that it will be understanding. In other words, poetry should carry us as far as it can beyond nature and the common man: it should carry us towards an ultimate goal which now seems like the ideal.

Mr MacDiarmid, although not interested in personal glory, wishes for his own poetry that it might arouse his race, that through it the world might find an outlet for what it has long been seeking. He is aware, however, that something within him is missing that will make possible such an achievement. In his youth he experienced sensations akin to those of Wordsworth in 'Tintern Abbey.' Earlier nature haunted him like a passion; then he changed. Regretfully he admits that he has fallen short of his goal, because although possessed of a live and passionate thought he has been unable to communicate it to the world. In theory Mr MacDiarmid's conception of poetry differs little from that of Wordsworth or Matthew Arnold. He realizes that a poem must not primarily be direct propaganda. One golden lyric is of more value than the solution of a particular social problem because it makes men less like apes and is a beacon light to the leaders, although 'they're owre blin' to see it.'

I have no quarrel with Mr MacDiarmid's general concep-

tion of the poet and poetry, or with his particular pronouncements. It is his application of these tenets that challenges the
reader of his work.[1] First, however, let us pursue our examination of the subject matter before attempting an evaluation of
his aesthetic achievement.

Patriotism, for example, is no empty flag-waving pseudo-
patriotism blinding him to his country's faults. It is a conviction that springs from his love of the very starkness of the
Scottish landscape, one whose infinite variety cannot be described in English words, a variety, however, with a basic
unity like that which he hopes underlies his own work, a basic
unity of spirit that he wants his countrymen to understand. He
reveals this aspect of his patriotism in 'The Little White Rose,'
and even more forcefully in the much longer 'Water Music.'
The reverse side of this aspect is his bitterness towards those
Scotsmen—expatriated or not—who speak of their love for
Scotland and yet passively see her decay. Among such are
those of the nobility who spend their substance in London,
many ecclesiastics who have lost the spirit of Christ, and selfish
politicians. Those who have most profited from her have been
her betrayers. The presence of tenements, hunger, and uncul-
tivated land attest the little that has been done in the past
hundred years. But not only have the leaders betrayed her!
Ninety per cent. of her sons have likewise done so. Since
much of the degradation of Scotland has resulted from her
union with England—when the Scots exchanged the great music
of the bagpipes for the English hurdy-gurdy—the only cure
lies in separation. He is, and he urges his fellow-countrymen to
be strong nationalists. No one can serve Scotland 'without
muckle trial and trouble to himsel'.[2]

[1] I have perhaps given too detailed a treatment of his pronouncements, and yet from
the frequency and the exhaustive treatment of this subject in his poetry it is evident that
the problem is one of his vital concerns.

[2] This aspect of his patriotism is, according to one of my Scottish friends, the sentimental reactions of a typical highlander. It is the lowlander that is the practical person.
According to such a classification Mr MacDiarmid would seem to be a combination of
both elements.

Inasmuch as Mr MacDiarmid carries his convictions to the point of a religious fervour it is little wonder that he finds little spiritual companionship among his relatives. A prophet is perforce a nuisance to his own family. The love-religion, he declares, has nowhere had a harder struggle than in Scotland, whose people, unfortunately, have fought in all the sham fights of the world, but have not fought the more important fight with themselves. Until they do, however, there is no hope for them, nor can there be anything in common between him and his countrymen. In his 'Lament for the Great Music' he not only urges the Scotsman to carry on his great tradition of culture, but makes a natural transition from the more immediate aspect of his patriotism to its larger aspect as manifested in the following pronouncement on his political ideology:

I am horrified by the triviality of life, by its corruption
    and helplessness,
No prospect of eternal life, no fullness of existence, no
    love without betrayal,
No passion without satiety. Yet life could be beautiful
    even now.
But all is soiled under philistine rule . . .

Yet there is no great problem in the world to-day
Except disease and death men cannot end
If no man tries to dominate another.

He disagrees with those economists who believe that the traditional economics is the only valid system. He is at odds with those religionists who in order to maintain the *status quo* present the concept of an anthropomorphic God. He bolsters his position in the straightforward 'First Objectives' by voicing his determination to eliminate class distinctions, war, capitalism, the church—all those things, in other words, that repress rather than point the way to a fuller life. That person who admonishes us to 'hold-have a care,' and who thereby prevents us from experiencing the soul quality of enjoying the 'divine in human or human in divine' is our natural enemy. He is everywhere about us; he is the upholder of a wrong concept of the aims of man and of the universe. The glory of mankind lies to-day where it has ever lain—in the goodness, simplicity, and patience of the vast majority of persons. Man can have what he wants and what is his due if he will only free himself from the antiquated concept of economics and will realize that his class, not the so-called upper classes, possesses the power. In fact, the life force needs the lowly things if it needs anything at all. It has little use for those of the idle leisure class.

Mr MacDiarmid is indignant at those who toady to royalty and is vitriolic against the abuses of capitalism. If to insist upon every man's right to the physical and spiritual values of life be communistic, then he is an ardent communist. Like most of the young poets and some of the so-called radical political leaders he believes that *laissez faire* is a thing of the past and that equality of opportunity must be provided for all. His admiration for Lenin lies in Lenin's insistence upon such a concept. In spite of any criticism that might be levelled against Lenin's methods, the fundamental fact remains that it is the thing done that counts, not how it is done. Had not the powers of Life and Thought been misused for the many, Lenin's methods would have been unnecessary. With a man's work to do Lenin behaved like a man and not like a child as most of us have been doing. After all, what does it matter whom we kill if it will 'lessen the foulest murder that deprives maist men o' real lives.'

Mr MacDiarmid has little patience with bibliolaters or with those who cloak love and religion in mysteries. The two are 'naked and unashamed,' and should be so treated. Why deny them, or why defame them? The Scotch religion particularly, with its traditional gloominess, is a woesome sight devoid of vitality. Like so much formal religion it has denied the principles of Christ. Most of the so-called professing

Christians—like the church itself—are greedy and self-seeking. They find smugness in the belief of Christ's sacrifice for mankind. Such fools are ever ready to give their opinions on God, life, death, and other mysteries. It is only the wise man who, aware of his own limitations, is willing to postpone all such thoughts. Why, he asks, be anxious about the future? Anyone who has come 'from sperm to maturity' has undergone so many changes that he need fear no more; his limits are determined by himself. Mr MacDiarmid, himself a great admirer of Christ, is essentially a mystic in his approach to the problem of God, and believes that truths greater than rationalistic ones spring from the subconscious mind. 'A Dog's Life' and 'An Apprentice Angel' are interesting side lights on his general thought.

He realizes that where there is too much talk about souls and God there is apt to be too little of the real spirit. 'Prayer for a Second Flood,' like so many of his poems with a religious cast, is essentially political in essence. It is a plea for a broader humanity. A striking quality of contemporary poetry is, in fact, the spirit of revolt from a religion whose essence is form and whose priests constitute a hierarchy of privilege in favour of a practical application of the golden rule. I do not believe that the average American reader has any conception of the thoughtful young Britisher's attitude towards the established church.

Mr MacDiarmid is aware, as many of his fellow enthusiasts are not, but as Lawrence certainly was, that it is almost impossible for the intellectual to become one with the working classes. Theoretically, one can talk about becoming one, but their body smells, their insensitivity, and their coarseness frequently repel the would-be fraternizer. But no vicarious living among them is possible. The artist must go beyond the borderline to the actual association. At present Mr MacDiarmid thinks that Russia probably provides the best opportunities for intimate contacts with the masses. A direct contact is, of course, often disillusioning to the idealist, but only by direct contact can one learn to understand the masses. Mr Eliot's failure to follow Mr MacDiarmid's suggestion is the cause of the fundamental falsity of many of the Sweeney poems as well as of a large bulk of 'The Waste Land.' Mr MacDiarmid is not so much an idealist or wishful thinker that he holds the workers themselves blameless. He realizes, as did Lawrence, that the conditions of the workers are 'due maistly to their ain mob cowardice'; that the workers are decidedly *not* inherently noble; that even with every opportunity for a full life they do not know how to grasp it; that they are not as equal to life as they are to the machines they tend; and that did they make a concerted effort they could achieve a change in a short time. In 'Reflections in an Ironworks' it is almost as if Lawrence himself were speaking:

> Would you resembled the metal you work with,
> Would the iron entered into your souls,
> Would you became like steel on your own behalf!
> You are still only putty that tyranny rolls
> Between its fingers! You makers of bayonets and guns
> For your own destruction! No wonder that those
> Weapons you make turn on you and mangle and murder—
> You fools who equip your otherwise helpless foes!

Mr MacDiarmid also echoes Lawrence in the lesson to be derived from this knowledge. We must not have our work as the end-all; rather we should be constantly striving not only to discover the meaning of life, but to find ways for bringing greater significance to it. We must not expect too much from the masses until we free them from the necessity of submitting to a regimen for the sake of their daily bread. But we cannot expect too much from the 'haves,' because those whose ancestors came by their wealth dishonestly 'are aye strang on the law.' Mr MacDiarmid understands their position, but regrets

it. Were man free from the tradition which has not only en-
slaved him in the past, but enslaves him now, he could attain
far greater heights than are at present possible. He could understand life as he cannot now do, because he would open the way
for greater experiences, the source of a knowledge of life:

> Nae man can ken his hert until
> The tide o' life uncovers it,
> And horror-struck he sees a pit
> Returnin' life can never fill.

Unfortunately, however, no evolution in self-knowledge has
occurred: the essential life of mankind in the mass is still the
same as that of their earliest ancestors. In all other fields the
world's ideas up to those of three hundred years ago have been
discarded. Would man only realize that did the methods in
mental advance approach those for material achievement the
rewards might possibly be as great! But the poor public will
swallow anything as long as it is sugar-coated!

Self-knowledge and an understanding of the meaning of life
are frequent themes in Mr MacDiarmid's poetry. We must
learn our lessons from the stones which alone are immutable.
After all:

> What happens to us
> Is irrelevant to the world's geology
> But what happens to the world's geology
> Is not irrelevant to us.

In fact, self-knowledge can come only from an intimate contact with life and with death. 'A man never faced wi' death,' he
says, 'kens nocht of life.'[1] The prostitute enlists his sympathy as
she has that of so many poets. To him as to them she is a symbol rather than a person. By serving Man, not merely a man,
she has a greater place than a sweetheart, wife, or mother, be-

---

[1]This tendency to view life and death as complementary probably derives from his
reading of Rainer Maria Rilke.

cause unlike them she cannot shut her life to Life. 'O Wha's Been Here Afore Me, Lass' presents another aspect of the same problem.[1] Once man has reached the limits of self-knowledge he must have the courage to make his world on the basis of his discovery in spite of the jeers of others. Only then can he hope to extend the process of self-knowledge to new limits.

Although he does not treat love as a routine subject, Mr MacDiarmid does not neglect it. Many beautiful lyrics in the early volumes and occasional ones in the later volumes reveal tenderness, passion, and understanding. A mother's love which not only differs markedly from that of a father, but reveals an essential quality of woman, is the subject of 'The Two Parents.' A mother's love, even towards a child born out of wedlock, can bring more joy than sorrow. 'The Robber,' for example, tells the same story as told by Hardy in 'The Dark-Eyed Gentleman.'

Interesting, however, as is the subject matter of a poet, its importance lies not only in the obvious control which it exercises on the music of the verse, but also in the subtlety it lends to certain aspects of that music. No poem has ever survived solely because of its intellectual content, whereas many poems of little or no intellectual content have achieved immortality. Some of Shakespeare's lyrics should quiet the sceptic. Let us look, therefore, at those aspects of Mr MacDiarmid's work which will determine his position as a poet.

I have already mentioned that Mr MacDiarmid writes both in Scots dialect and in English, the former predominating in the earlier volumes and the latter elsewhere. His Scots dialect is of no one locality as Burns' was that of Ayrshire; but he selects, according to Mr John Buchan, 'where he pleases between Aberdeen and the Cheviots.' This boldness has made many of the pieces difficult for the reader. Moreover, and this was to be expected of a man using a new weapon, he has often failed. No one likes to have constant recourse to a glossary;

[1] The poems in this genre bear a striking resemblance to many by Hardy.

and even then, those he provides are incomplete. The general idea of the poem is clear enough, but an accurate perception of the poet's intention is impossible. The reader is left unsatisfied. I do not mean to give the impression that this is always the case. Were it so, there would be no meaning to the present essay. 'The Watergaw,' 'The Bonnie Broukit Bairn,' 'Water Music,' 'Wheesht, Wheesht,' the delightfully satiric 'Crowdie-knowe,' and innumerable others are undoubted successes. Unlike Burns, Mr MacDiarmid can write in English with the same force, often with a greater one, than in Scots. 'The Herd of Does,' for example, has all the lyric intensity of any of the dialect poems. By tending to simplify his Scots diction in his later volumes I think Mr MacDiarmid will win a wider circle of readers than was before possible.

A second characteristic that troubles the American reader is the frequent ornateness and heavy latinity of his diction. The Scots have always had a predilection for rhetoric, and no less a scholar than Professor Nichol Smith of Oxford, himself a Scotsman, has remarked on the Scots' delight in using erudite words.[1] As a matter of fact, it is frequently impossible to believe that Mr MacDiarmid can be serious. Instead of a preponderance of monosyllables, polysyllabic words abound. The objection to this practice is not on account of the length of the words, but on account of the faulty communication that results. Not only is the basic or traditional rhythm of English poetry disturbed, but these aureate words carry for us no emotional connotation derived from past associations; no more, in fact, than do the unfamiliar Scots words of literary origin. In 'Vestigia Nulla Retrorsum (In Memoriam: Rainer Maria Rilke 1875–1926)' at least thirty-seven strange words confront even

---

[1] 'To the present day the Scottish student dearly loves a well-rounded resounding sentence. . . . We are apt to forget the large place occupied by Latin in vernacular Scots. Latin was at one time as familiar to the educated Scot as his mother-tongue, and was his means of communication with foreigners. The Scot abroad made his way with Latin. The Scottish authors who were known abroad wrote in Latin. Scots Law, which is founded on Roman Law, has a larger Latin element than English Law. Latin words were bound to creep into the vernacular. More than that, Latin words have come into English from Scottish usage.' *Some Aspects of Eighteenth Century Poetry*

an enlightened reader.[1] What happens is, of course, the complete loss of lyricism in such passages. 'Ephyphatha,' stressing the alliteration on 'p' and 'f,' is another instance in kind. Perhaps to the Scottish ear the presence of such words does not present a bar to the musical pattern; but to an American ear the result differs little from the effect produced by an ultra-modern musical composition in a totally unfamiliar idiom. 'Stony Limits' is a striking example of Mr MacDiarmid's practice. Written as a memorial to Charles Doughty (1843–1927), a man whose ways were different from those of the poet, it has a nobility which is enhanced by the images as well as by the sheer music of the verse; but again the learned diction jars on the ear of the reader accustomed to the diction of traditional English poetry. I am, of course, not concerned with the possible reaction of future generations to Mr. MacDiarmid's aureate and erudite vocabulary. Fortunately, these experiments, because I do not think they can be anything more, are confined chiefly to *Stony Limits*. They do not reappear in *Second Hymn to Lenin and Other Poems*.

Mr MacDiarmid's figurative language transcends the merely picturesque. 'Prayer for a Second Flood,' a strongly satiric poem showing traces of what A.E. called 'the sardonic rebel' contains figures that are unusual, striking, and keyed to the tone of the poem. Of the numerous Noahs of to-day who speak with confidence of the ways of the Lord, he says:

Ding a' their trumpery show to bauds again.
Their measure is the thimblefu' o' Esk in spate.

[1]The following are a few: Halophilous, cleistogamic, abreption, abderian, accidie, gynandromorphic, lectisternium, immarcescible, and laevorotatory. One stanza will illustrate the difficulty:

In shades of lastery and filemot and gridelin,
Stammel and perse, our chesil and turbary lie
Far from Scotland, that land of liripoops we left
    On these sterile stones, all else bereft,
To watch the lacertine gleams, the lightning hummers, still.
Nature with her excessive being no more could come
Over us here, we thought, as prophecy over Paul;
Lagophthalmic as God himself we yet descry
Overwhelming nimiety in this minimum!

Like whiskey the tittlin' craturs mete oot your poo'ers
Aince a week for baubees in the kirk-door plate,
—And pit their umbrellas up when they come oot
    If mair than a pulpitfu' o' You's aboot!

The imagery in 'At My Father's Grave' is likewise arresting:

The sunlict still on me, you row'd in clood,
We look upon each ither noo like hills
Across a valley. I'm nae mair your son.
It is my mind, nae son o' yours, that looks,
And the great darkness o' your death comes up
And equals it across the way.
A livin' man upon a deid man thinks
And ony sma'er thocht's impossible.

But in spite of his insistence on thought Mr MacDiarmid realizes that some of the greatest experiences lie beyond the poet's ability to crystallize them in language. The true poet speaks in 'As Lovers Do':

Here at the height of passion
    As lovers do
I can only speak brokenly
    Of trifles too.

Idiot incoherence
    I know full well
Is the only language
    That with God can deal.

But what he frequently fails to realize is that metrical dialectic is not poetry. He is so carried away by his convictions, so eager to raise the reader to his same pitch of intense emotion that he fails. Too often his verses communicate the sense of nervous energy without communicating the sense of passion. They have a matter-of-factness that disturbs the reader. One never doubts whether or not he has thought intensely about his matter; but one does doubt whether or not he has thought equally intensely about the dress of those thoughts. It seems to me that many poems are only prose broken up into a metrical pattern. It is possible, however, that he has not considered it worth his while to labour in polishing one thought when other thoughts were crowding his mind. But if that is true, I think he has seriously erred. Like Donne he is interested in communicating the subtleties developing from his main idea rather than in making the main idea all powerful. No one can deny that Mr MacDiarmid is intellectually stimulating. He bludgeons the old orthodoxies with the club of a zealot and poses problems the solution of which demands of us our best.

But I do not wish to leave the reader with the idea that he is incapable of genuine song. I have already mentioned several fine lyrics. Stately music and searching thought combine in 'On a Raised Beach.' The nightingale lyric in 'Circumjack Cencrastus,' 'Dytiscus,' and the 'Ballad of Five Senses,' to mention but a few, attain a high level of achievement. They are no less thoughtful than his other poems, but they present Mr MacDiarmid as a thinker *and* a poet.

Several factors conspire to prevent Mr MacDiarmid from achieving popularity in America in the way that the Messrs Auden, Spender, MacNeice, and Day Lewis have achieved it. His use of dialect is one, the hardness of his thought, his frequent matter-of-factness, and his refusal to seek popularity are others. He is willing to await the response to his poetry. It would, however, be an injustice to Mr MacDiarmid as well as to the other men to attempt to weigh one against the other. What Mr Spender has said of himself is true, I believe, of every sincere poet: 'One does not try to be greater or better than other writers, one is trying to be as truthful as one can and we should be judged by the limits of that truth set against the greater truth of others.' The clothing of Mr MacDiarmid's thoughts bears no resemblance to that of the poets I have already mentioned—it is the difference between Harris tweed and West-of-England cloth. But the thoughts are frequently striking in their similarity. One thing is certain. To all classes with their increasing awareness to social problems and their revision of their views of life as science has pushed back the boundaries of the universe Mr MacDiarmid has much to say and he says it with force. One may cavil at individual poems, one may disagree violently with specific ideas; but when one lays aside the volumes of his work and thinks about his accomplishment one realizes he has been in the presence of a man of erudition steeped in the best thought of the past and the present if not always in the presence of a great poet; that he has been in the presence of a man who by sincerity of expression, by subtlety and keenness of intellect, and by indomitable energy has sought to fire his readers to an adequate perception of the universe, of our immediate world and its needs, and of their place therein.

CECIL DAY LEWIS

INTERESTING as are the revolutionary aspects of Mr Day Lewis's poetry, even more so is the story of their genesis and evolution. In the final analysis the value of his work will lie in the manner in which he tells that story; not in the political conclusions at which he arrived. His political ideology is frequently naïve; not so are those of love, beauty, and ambition. More important than his ideas, however, are the rich and diverse borrowings from nature for the illumination of his ideas. His is the predicament of a man standing between two worlds torn by his loyalties to each. Because he so deeply loves the best qualities of his natural heritage he will support a revolution in order that all may share the joys of that heritage.

His revolution of society aims at the liberation of the English underdog and a reduction of the excessive privileges of the aristocracy. Every class must have equal opportunities. Lawrence pounded at this idea in *Last Poems*. Before Lawrence others had put forward the same idea both in poetry and prose. To-day the subject is the common property of the group of poets of which Mr Day Lewis is a member.

Progress has been made, but the conditions existing a century ago seemed no worse to the men of that day than do those of to-day seem to men like Mr Day Lewis. Fulke Greville, himself a member of the privileged class, has given us a picture of English society that is still essentially true to-day. He wrote in 1829:

> Poverty and vice and misery must always be found in a community like ours, but such frightful contrasts between the excess of luxury and splendour and these scenes of starvation and brutality ought not to be possible; but I am afraid there is more vice, more misery and penury in this country than in any other, and at the same time greater

wealth. The contrasts are too striking, and such an unnatural, artificial and unjust state of things neither can nor ought to be permanent. I am convinced that before many years elapse these things will produce some great convulsion.

'Convulsion' is too emotional a word to describe the great social changes that have already taken place; 'mutations' would be better. It is, however, the word that Mr Day Lewis and his friends use to describe the means by which the social ameliora-tion of the under-privileged for which they are working will be accomplished. The evolution of Mr Day Lewis's awareness of the necessity for change, the statement of his aims, and the pro-cesses by which those aims may be accomplished are the sub-ject-matter of his poetry.

He enunciates his general principles in *Transitional Poem*, gives frequent concrete examples of them in *From Feathers to Iron*, the poem dealing with the birth of his son, elaborates his ideas in *The Magnetic Mountain*, adds significant details in some shorter poems of the volume *A Time to Dance*, attempts a symphonic synthesis of them in the title poem, *A Time to Dance*, and re-states them in the idiom of the morality play in *Noah and the Waters*,[1] and clothes them in better poetry in *Overtures to Death*. Since *The Magnetic Mountain* Mr Day Lewis has done little except (by a re-statement of his ideas in different forms) to solidify his position.

The poet traces his emergence from the period of adolescent emotional pessimism to the period of sound thinking. It is the story of a thoughtful youth. No metamorphosis occurred. Be-cause he possessed the lively sensibility of the poet, the change was more marked in him than in the average boy; but it was the result of normal processes—of the impact of four persons

[1] I think it is important to note that *Transitional Poem*, *From Feathers to Iron*, and *The Magnetic Mountain* are in reality three cycles of short or comparatively short lyrics. *Transitional Poem* is divided into 34 closely related sections; *From Feathers to Iron* into 29; and *The Magnetic Mountain*, into 36. *A Time to Dance* follows the form of a symphony with its several movements, its statement of diverse themes, and the elaboration and recapitula-tion, closing with a finale in the classic manner.

on a sensitive mind. A girl, by changing his lust to love, increased his comprehension; a philosopher, by teaching him dialectic, clarified his thinking and strengthened his reasoning powers; a harlot broadened his understanding of man; and a poet taught him that truths frequently result from inspiration. The result was, of course, inevitable. Discontent and ambition forced him out of himself to seek from a close contact with reality the underlying unity and harmony of the universe. His experiences, by leading him to probe the nature and power of desire, convinced him that it was the mind and not the heart that was credulous, and that only the inhabitants of the Ivory Tower (who see with the mind, not the heart) can be deluded into thinking that the deplorable social and political conditions are tolerable.

The poet, unable to find a rational explanation of the world, does not find the expanding universe made possible by science less wonderful or enthralling than the limited conception of an older generation. True wisdom or an understanding of the universe, possible only through sensuous and mystic sensation, requires a warm multiple personality disciplined by thought and expression. Truth cannot, therefore, be found in solitude. It is possible only in the 'blind collisions' constantly present in city life, and then only to the person who knows every inch of the way, not only the high spots. This realization forced him to discard the traditional beliefs associated with the leisured class to which he belonged.

To strike out boldly and independently required courage, particularly in an age of 'a fevered head and a cold heart' where the rulers are incapable, where those who are dissatisfied will do nothing to alleviate their dissatisfaction, and where the masses with power in their hands do not know how to be great. For his son's sake, however, he was willing to engage in the struggle for the creation of a new order, to alter the conditions under which in order to prosper a man must surrender his independence and intellectual integrity.

The task was not easy and Mr Day Lewis communicates to us the constant struggle he waged with conflicting emotional and mental loyalties. The quiet leisured life far from the conflicts between capital and labour was pleasant to him; but, believing that anyone who attempted neutrality would be crushed, that some choice was necessary, he cast his life with the workers. His sympathies and tastes inclined him to the old order; logically and intellectually he was of the new order. Reason won. It was, and is, the poet's belief that those who are fortunate in their positions in life, who have had the advantages and have also achieved great things, have lost sight of reality. They are not aware that the under-privileged workers, having received no share in the benefits, are becoming restless. Mr Day Lewis, seeking a broadened humanity, exposes the obstacles to its achievement. He implies that a general application should be made from his own experience.

Four defendants of the traditional order impede his progress: his mother, 'public school' education, formalized religion, and his wife. He acknowledges his debt to his mother for his early training, but rebels against her possessive instinct and insists that he be permitted to live his own life. Public school education is outmoded, is blind to strange or new ideas, stifles enthusiasm, and breeds a disinterested attitude toward suffering. The church has been wholly selfish in its aims; it has not championed the cause of the poor. His wife, believing that love should be enough, is unable to recognize that love is but a part of his life. The more important part, forever shut off from her, is the solitude in which his spirit struggles upwards.

Four enemies actively resist the advent of the new order: sex, the press, lack of faith, and the rejection of the active life. Man must overcome these before his spiritual nature can dominate his material one. Woman is the eternal Circe; the press 'dopes' the masses and panders to their overweening love of the sensational; the systematic faith-lacking approach to religion prevents man from seeking God in nature and in the crises of life; the poet who lacks pride and a sense of power and who fails to remain in the fight (although not he but future generations reap the benefits) is as great an enemy as any.

Until Part IV of *The Magnetic Mountain* we have no positive statement of what must be done. The poet has given us with less detail than did Wordsworth in *The Prelude* an autobiographical account of his early mental and emotional development from boyhood to maturity and of his increasing awareness of the forces preventing mankind from achieving complete fulfilment. Anyone who expects a practical working plan from Mr Day Lewis will be disappointed. He has no right to expect it.

I have dealt thus at length with *The Magnetic Mountain* because in it he states his ideas more fully than elsewhere in his poetry, not because it is his best poem.

Mr Day Lewis is not the 'hierophant of an unapprehended inspiration'; he has simply attempted a poetical treatment of the intellectual ideas made current by Bertrand Russell, C. E. M. Joad, Walter Lippman, D. H. Lawrence, and others. His work is of his age. He believes that man has gone at so fast a pace that he needs a saviour, someone who has freed himself of all encumbrances. The followers of this saviour must be men who will sacrifice private income from investment and will be prepared to share alike, who must boldly break with the tradition whose roots are in a vanished era. These men will come from three major divisions of the population: those who love England in her natural beauty and seek refuge in her rural scenes; those who like people, are happy in a small way, and have escaped disaster; and those who have suffered beyond endurance.

These will possess the world, a co-operative commonwealth. Since, however, life is short they must act quickly. A revolution is necessary; but to be successful it must not be over-hasty. The temper of the people must first undergo a change. When conditions have been ameliorated and the big issues settled then can there be a return to sports, love, and individual achievement.

It is evident, I think, that what Mr Day Lewis gives us is a more detailed examination of the source of his discontent than we find elsewhere in poetry. The history of the development of his mind is as important, if not more so, than his ideology. His attitude toward traditional institutions—that of a sensitive young man who after a protected youth is startled and horrified when he comes in contact with reality—is understandable. As a picture of his mind and of the minds of many in the so-called leftist-labour group his poetry is frequently of great value. It is unfortunate that in his attempt to communicate his ideas he is often dull and prosy. His solution of the difficulty by revolution is, in the manner of Shelley, youthful and naïve. For a practical working solution, his ideas are vaguely stated, hopelessly idealistic. When he can be calm with a calmness which is the result of a carefully controlled emotion, his poetry can be of definite value to that ever-increasing group which feels that every man has a right to more than a mere physical subsistence; but, and perhaps rightly so, its value will lie in its heartening powers rather than in a definite plan of procedure.

Mr Day Lewis's treatment of love is direct. It is also unique in English literature. His fresh treatment of this old subject has been overlooked by the majority of his critics. At no time does false sentimentality mar his work. His is the honesty found in such poems as Meredith's *Modern Love*.[1] *From Feathers to Iron*, for example, is a minute record of the subtleties in the psychological attitudes of husband and wife to one another and to the prospective child from the period immediately preceding her pregnancy until the birth of their son.

Modern, too, is his attitude toward beauty. It can be found anywhere—even in a muddy canal:

[1] I refer the reader to the following poems should he wish to corroborate my statement: *Transitional Poem*, sections 5, 19, 21, 22, 23, 26, 27; *From Feathers to Iron*, the entire poem, particularly sections 23 and 24; *Noah and the Waters* in *A Time to Dance*, page 143.

This glum canal has lain
Opaque night after night
One hour will entertain
A jubilee of light
And show that *beauty is*
A motion of the mind
By its own dark caprice
Directed or confined.
(*Transitional Poem*, Section 30)

Each new generation finds it in new forms, in strange places:

Beauty breaks ground, O, in strange places.
Seen after cloudburst down the bone-dry watercourses,
In Texas a great gusher, a grain-
Elevator in the Ukraine plain;
To a new generation turns new faces.
(*From Feathers to Iron*, Section XXVI)

His attitude toward fame and greatness is sensible. To achieve immortality one should do as did Ulysses, Herodotus, Columbus, and others—mind 'one's own business magnanimously,' and see important meanings in every day events:

To find a holiday
In the sticks and mud
Of a familiar road
(*Transitional Poem*, Section 10)

II

I have already mentioned that even more important than his ideas is the rich and abundant use Mr Day Lewis makes of nature for the communication of those ideas. In his nature poetry and in those images drawn from nature he is a good poet carrying on the tradition of a great and abiding class of English poetry. In the presence of nature he does not have to lash himself into a fury of indignation at social abuse. He is calm, deeply moved, and reflective. The expression of this deeply spiritual attitude in his poetry invests it with passionate intensity. It marks him as a true poet.

It is a truism that the beauties of the English landscape have inspired such a body of nature poetry as is found in no other country. Mr Day Lewis has assimilated the many phases of the tradition. These blend and fuse in his work. Nature induces in him a mystic attitude, serves in a symbolic capacity for his ideas of man and the universe, heightens the communication of his setting, is a source of images which vivify ideas that would otherwise remain inarticulate, and inspires him to first-rate descriptive poetry. No contemporary poet is more steeped in nature than he. He follows the tradition of Thomson and of Wordsworth rather than of Cowper.

He is a mystic, for example, when at dusk—

> In that one moment of evening
> When roses are most red
> I can fold back the firmament,
> I can put time to bed—
>
> (*Transitional Poem*, Section 4)

he has 'an instant realized,' when he can grasp the significance and meaning of the universe better than he could with a lifetime of experience. Although rare, the value of such moments cannot be over-estimated.

At times, however, when the mind absorbed in 'its own forked speculation' attempts by a return to nature to free itself of the storm that besets it, it cannot, like Wordsworth—even in the hills of the lake district—find any balm, any comfort in her. Rationalization is no help. How can he attain to the sublimity of the mountains when even they who are above the world want to be of it! But at times, nature does exert a soothing power over him. In the crowds, obsessed with the problems

of when 'systems . . . that include the man' will come into
being, nature heartens him. . . .

> Then I remember the pure and granite hills
> Where first I caught an ideal tone that stills,
> Like the beloved's breath asleep, all din
> Of earth at traffic . . .

(Transitional Poem, Section 14)

Before the birth of his son, it exerts a similar influence. In
From Feathers to Iron, the nature images accurately reflect the
poet's changing moods before and during the period of his
wife's pregnancy. Fresh similes in which he compares her to
the white rose and the poplar reveal her character and, perhaps
even more, his. He sees, too, in the woman's condition a
parallel to the returning spring:

> Earth wears a smile betrays
> What summer she has in store.
> She feels insurgent forces
> Gathering at the core,
> And a spring of rumour courses
> Through her, till the cold extreme
> Sleep of grove and grass is
> Stirred, begins to dream.

Observe, too, how he communicates the father's joy, pride,
and eagerness over the approach of the child's birth:

> Now the full-throated daffodils,
> Our trumpeters in gold,
> Call resurrection from the ground
> And bid the year be bold.

> To-day the almond tree turns pink
> The first flush of the spring;
> Winds loll and gossip through the town
> Her secret whispering . . .

(Section XIV 'Now the full-throated daffodils')

At such times, too, nature does bring comfort:

> I see the mating plover at play
> Blowing themselves about over the green wheat,
> And in a bank I catch
> The shy scent of the primrose that prevails
> Strangely upon the heart. Here is
> The last flutter of the wind-errant soul,
> Earth's first faint tug at the earthbound soul.
> So, waiting here between winter and summer,
> Conception and fruition, I
> Take what refreshment may be had from skies
> Uncertain as the wind, prepare
> For a new route, a change of constitution.
>   (Section XV, 'I have come so far
>   upon my journey')

More important, however, is the way Mr Day Lewis employs nature images to interpret his every thought. He does not write of nature simply because he loves her, but because by so doing he can clarify, bolster, and strengthen by comparison and contrast his communication of the protagonists' minds. We feel the father's pride in the child about to be born—

> Now too the bird must try his voice
> Upon the morning air;
> Down drowsy avenues he cries
> A novel great affair.
> He tells of royalty to be . . .

The child (Section XVIII, 'It is time to think of you'), even though it come to a world that is 'essential dark,' will be—

> As anemones that renew
> Earth's innocence, be welcome.
> Out of your folded sleep
> Come, as the western winds come
> To pasture with the sheep
> On a weary of winter heights.

The harvest (Section XX, 'Sky-wide an estuary of light') provides an analogue to his wife's loss of beauty and agility—a loss, however, for which the child will be adequate compensation. The heaviness of his own mind at the thought that his wife might die in child-birth is reflected in the heaviness of the summer season. (Section XXVII, 'Dropping the few last days, are drops of lead.')

Not only in such moods, however, do nature images vitalize his thought. In *The Magnetic Mountain* (Section 8, 'This was your world and this I owe you') he paints a sensuous, appealing picture of nature in order to make his break with a tradition with which he could no longer sympathize necessitate the greater courage. He definitely bolsters his political idea (Section 28, 'Though winter's barricade delays') by reflecting the new movement in the rebellious attitude of spring against winter—

> Though winter's barricade delays,
> Another season's in the air;
> We'll sow the spring in our young days,
> Found a Virginia everywhere.
>
> Look where the ranks of crocuses
> Their rebel colours will display
> Coming with quick fire to redress
> The balance of a wintry day.
>
> Those daffodils that from the mould
> Drawing a sweet breath soon shall flower,
> With a year's labour got their gold
> To spend it on a sunny hour...

Passages of sensuous nature descriptions abound. Quotation is difficult. They are, moreover, as I have already mentioned, closely bound up with his thought pertaining to problems of man. Impressive, however, seem to me many of the stanzas from *Johnny-Head-In-Air*, particularly the description of his face—

His face was pure as the *winnowed* light
When the wild geese fly high,
And gentle as on October evenings
The heron-feathered sky—

(*Johnny Head-in-Air*)

and there is a largeness which almost teases us out of thought in the following picture of dusk!

Sky-wide an estuary of light
Ebbs amid cloud banks out of sight.
At her *star-anchorage* shall swing
Earth, the old freighter, till morning.

(*From Feathers to Iron*, Section XX)

Mr Day Lewis does not confine his description to static phenomena. He can catch the movement of clouds or crystallize the emotion connected with the approaching storm in the manner of Shelley—

Chiefly to mind appears
That hour on Silverhowe
When evening's lid hung low
And the sky was about our ears.
Buoyed between fear and love
We watched in eastward form
The armadas of the storm
And sail superbly above;
So near, they'd split and founder
On the least jag of sense,
One false spark fire the immense
Broadside the confounding thunder.

(*Transitional Poem*, Section 26)

A passage in *The Magnetic Mountain* using musical terminology achieves a quieter but more complete picture of the beauty that is England:

You that love England, who have an ear for her music,
The slow movement of clouds in benediction,
Clear arias of light thrilling over her uplands,
Over the chords of summer sustained peacefully;
Ceaseless the leaves' counterpoint in a west wind lively,
Blossom and river rippling loveliest allegro,
And the storms of wood strings brass at year's finale:
Listen. Can you not hear the entrance of a new theme?

It is already evident from the foregoing selections that the poet appreciates the use of forceful epithet in the communication of his ideas. He surprises his readers by combining apparently antithetic elements into forceful images—at times elaborated into a sustained simile or metaphor, at others concentrated into a single word. This ability, the basis of his poetic power, reveals a controlled but rich poetic imagination. With the lighting of a fire, for example, 'the hedge of darkness sprang up like a bean stalk by which our Jack aspired once.' Dogs play a frequent rôle in his similes of dawn, the wind, prairie fire:

A. Dawn like a greyhound leapt the hill-tops.
(*The Magnetic Mountain*, Section 8)
B. The red nor'-easter is out:
Trees in the covert strain
Like dogs upon a leash
And snuff the hurricane.
(*Transitional Poem*, Section 32)

C. . . . I have seen flames browsing
On the prairie of night and tossing
Their muzzles up at Orion.
(*Transitional Poem*, Section 20)

Birds, too, help to illumine the poet's mental states. At one time, he says,

I felt, in my scorning,
Of common poet's talk,

> As arrogant as the hawk
> When he mounts above the morning;
> > (*Transitional Poem*, Section 1)

At another:

> Peals of the New Year once for me came tumbling
> Out of the narrow night like clusters of humming-
> Birds loosed from a black bag, and rose again
> Irresponsibly to silence: but now I strain
> To follow them and see for miles around
> Men square or shrug their shoulders at the sound.
> > (*Transitional Poem*, Section 14)

The ardour of love finds expression in a simile of the elms:

> When in love's airs we'd lie
> Like elms we leaned together with a sigh
> And sighing severed, and no rest
> Had till that wind was past:
> Then dropped in green sickness over the plain
> Wanting our wind again.
> > (*From Feathers to Iron*, Section XIII)

We feel the consternation of a man trapped in a quarry by a fall of rock when

> Nightmare nags at his elbow and narrows
> Horizon to pinpoint, hope to hand's breadth,
> Slow drip the seconds, time is stalactite.
> > (*From Feathers to Iron*, Section XII)

Single epithets frequently crystallize a particular movement of nature and its attending emotion. The following lines, for example, would lose much were any other words substituted for 'matriarch' and 'draggled'; they are right:

> Could I be child again
> And grip those skirts of cloud the matriarch sky
> Draggled on mere and hillside?
> > (*Transitional Poem*, Section 6)

The sensuousness of the scene on Lillington Common is heightened by 'wallowed':

> That afternoon we lay on Lillington Common
> The land wallowed around us in the sunlight.
>
> (*Transitional Poem*, Section 3)

When he speaks of the 'purple rhetoric of evening skies' a highly wrought sunset immediately flashes to mind. An insight into the writer's emotional nature is revealed by his 'Go not this road, for arc-lamps *cramp* the dawn.' He who has sat about a camp-fire readily grasps the truth of the image of darkness:

> ... yet was I lord of
> Something: for, seeing the fall of a burnt-out faggot
> Make all the night sag down, I became lord of
> Light's interplay—stoker of an old parable.
>
> (*Transitional Poem*, Section 3)

To speak of the wood lark's 'irrelevant song' or of the hauntings of death's 'black-bordered fancies' are further evidences of Mr Day Lewis's poetic power.

In his latest volume, *Overtures to Death*, the same qualities exist, but the imagery surprises by its greater freshness and its enhanced evocative qualities. When he speaks of the 'sequin glitter of leaves' in 'Landscapes'; of the colour of maple and sumach in autumn of such a scarlet character that

> For this their russet and rejoicing week
> Trees spend a year of sunsets on their pride:

of the swan

> Riding at her image, anchored there
> Complacent, a water-lily upon
> The ornamental water:

of the poet's 'earliest memory, the mood fingered and frail as maidenhair'; or of

> Self-pity like a thin rain fell,
> Fouling the view,

he communicates his mood to the reader more completely than he has yet done. He has effected no revolution in his prosody; but more than at any other time he has tended to load the rifts of his subject with ore.

Irony is an important ingredient in these later poems, as well as in the earlier. It is bitter in 'Newsreel,' 'Sex Crime,' and 'Night Piece'; it is slightly tempered in 'Regency Houses,' 'A Landscape,' and 'The Bells that Signed'; it is at its subtlest and best in the group of seven title lyrics. More clearly than any of the other poems in the volume and more poetically than in the preceding volumes this group reveals the attitude of the present generation of realists to its problems. He is political in a less expository and didactic way than in the earlier poems, but in that lies his greater universality. He no longer tells us about the problems of his adjustments to the political scene; he makes us share the problems with him.

'The Nabara,' a moving poem of an incident in the late Spanish war related in G. L. Steer's *The Tree of Gernika*, is in a different genre from the other poems. In the narrowest sense it is a narrative of an uneven battle between the plucky government trawlers Nabara, Guipuzkoa, Bizkaya, and Donostia and the rebel cruiser, Canarias. In the larger sense it is a memorial to those stalwart Basques to whom

> Freedom was more than a word, more than the base coinage
> Of politicians who hiding behind the skirts of peace
> They had defiled, gave up that country to rack and carnage,

and strikes the keynote of the volume, the problem of maintaining one's freedom in a distraught world.

III

At times, however, particularly in the early work, he spoils the force of his achievement by a too-conscious imitation of Mr

T. S. Eliot and others. 'Spoon out the waters of comfort in kilogrammes,' for example, derives directly from the 'I have measured out my life in coffee spoons' of Mr Alfred Prufrock. Mr Eliot's influence goes far deeper, however, than the similarity of an occasional image. Mr Day Lewis has in several instances assimilated his thought and poetic texture. Perhaps I should say has partially assimilated them, because it would be impossible for a poet of Mr Day Lewis's temperament to make a complete assimilation of so un-English a poet as Mr Eliot. Reverberations from *The Waste Land* beat too consistently upon the ear in 'On my right are trees and a lank stream sliding.' In his image of Phlebas and in his idea that the time has come for him to set his own house in order we have additional echoes of *The Waste Land*.

Rupert Brooke's *The Great Lover* dominates 'It is becoming now to declare my allegiance.' Yet there is a difference. The poem fortunately lacks Brooke's facility. It possesses, instead, more of the quality of Donne struggling to come to grips with his subject.

'Moving In' is directly in the tradition of Gerard Manley Hopkins. Quieter in mood than many, this poem is more effective because the spirit of indignation is more restrained. Hopkins and Owens fuse into a third voice in the passage 'Getters not begetters' (*The Magnetic Mountain*, Section 25). Shelley and Wordsworth, too, have had a share in shaping Mr Day Lewis's poetry. More unusual, however, is the influence of the popular song on sections of a poem the title of which is taken from *Ecclesiastes*! And Marlowe's 'Come live with me and be my love' is strangely metamorphosed into a poem of trenchant political irony.

I have no quarrel with the influences; I do object to their obviousness and the way in which they frequently mar the unity of his work. They are interesting as documentary evidence of the eclecticism of his interests. It is imperative, however, that a man so steeped in all schools of English poetry should effect a synthesis from which emerges a new voice. Several poems already attest that his work will not be a distorted reflection of others.

Mr Day Lewis has had recourse to many technical devices in order to communicate thought and emotion. In 'Make no mistake' (*The Magnetic Mountain*, Section 4) he makes frequent use of internal rhyme and unequal verse lengths to intensify the commonplaceness of the diction. The metre reflects the mediocrity of the majority of the passengers. In 'Let us now praise famous men' the metrical structure communicates the dryness, stiffness, the 'good form' of the public school product. No freedom or enthusiasm enlivens the verses. At other times he uses half rhymes effectively. His best work, however, is done in traditional metrical forms. 'Rest from loving and be living,' 'Come live with me,' 'It is becoming now to declare my allegiance,' 'Do not expect again the Phoenix hour,' 'Now she is like the white tree-rose,' and 'Chiefly to mind appears' are but a few examples.

IV

Mr Day Lewis is typically English in the restraint of his diction. It is passionate, yet never sensual. He possesses none of Mr Spender's oriental quality. His poetry, with the cleanness of an English landscape, is thoroughly impregnated with the love of liberty and of England which is the marrow of the finest English poetry. His work is, in fact, intensely patriotic; but patriotic in the same way in which Burns' poetry reveals his patriotism for Scotland. He does not wave a Union Jack and talk platitudes and at the same time scotch those who have been denied their English heritage. He denounces the rulers who have tried to deny the people their inalienable rights. He favours communism because he believes that under a communistic régime the masses will again come into their own.

His long poems are not wholly successful. *Transitional Poem*, *From Feathers to Iron*, and *The Magnetic Mountain*, being in reality a series of closely connected short poems, do not build up to one sustained emotion. *A Time to Dance*, which follows the symphonic form, is in spite of numerous excellent passages definitely weak. The opening is dull and prosy, and the end lacks unity. *Noah and the Waters*, alone of them all, tends, as it proceeds, to sustain, even to intensify, the emotional communication. It is also true, however, that no extracts from the shorter lyrics give an adequate conception of his achievement.

Power reveals itself in his work the moment he associates himself closely with nature; when, in other words, he lets the child be father to the man.

I cannot help thinking that as he emerges from his revolutionary period his work will grow immeasurably. When he refrains from lashing himself into a fury of indignation, he is a poet of the first magnitude—when, in other words, he follows his own advice and surrenders himself to his demon. *Overtures to Death* gives promise that he will do just that.

I should not like to see Mr Day Lewis lose his interest in the improvement of the condition of the under-privileged. I feel certain that every careful reader of his, Mr Spender's, and Mr Auden's work will never view with the same passivity the political problem demanding solution. It is only that he will move us more as his work reflects measured thought rather than youthful hysteria. In America, at least, our way of life is such that the average man comes in contact at an early age with the things that an English school boy does not encounter until he has left the university. He is not shocked, therefore, at an impressionable time of life. Since he can sympathize only with what his experience permits him to accept, he cannot sympathize with a too highly wrought expression of horror at social conditions.

The corpus of Mr Day Lewis's work that will possess more than historical interest is still very small. A few love poems and several nature poems impregnated with revolutionary ideas will undoubtedly find a permanent place in our literature. But he does not possess the lyric gift in the highest degree. With Mr Auden's poetry, for example, there are numerous poems in which one feels the diction is almost flawless; in his, never. I look forward to the time, however, when he puts into practice what he already knows about the danger of setting his political ideology above the problem of his technique. He has shown signs of this in *Noah and the Waters*. A poet must have something to say worth saying; but he must say it in a manner in which it has never before been said. Of the poet, he himself has written:

> His gaze that like the moonlight rests on all
> In level contemplation, making roof and ruin
> Treachery scorn and death into silver syllables
> And out of worn fragments a seamless coat.

He must not forget the 'silver syllables.'

WYSTAN HUGH AUDEN

THE award (November 23rd, 1937) of the King's Gold Medal for poetry to Mr Wystan Hugh Auden, thirty-year old poet and dramatist, pleased those who look upon him as the foremost of the younger English poets. The many who were annoyed at the award because they consider his work unintelligible need not greatly concern us. Mr Auden's early poetry is frequently difficult; but the difficulty lies less in his media of communication than with the experiences communicated. A poem is set down as vague which is only difficult. The difficulty lies neither in obscurity of expression nor in the presence of a private joke, but in his attempt at the communication of experiences which have rarely before been frankly dealt with in poetry. Criticism of his work has too often taken the form of a discussion of his prosodic skill as of something independent of his subject matter; but we cannot divorce the thing said from the way of saying it. In the following analysis of his poetic thought one must constantly remember that the technique by which he has communicated his ideas gives importance to the ideas themselves.

One can classify the two chief themes of Mr Auden's poetry in a number of ways: we might say Auden the Marxist and Auden the Freudian; or Auden the observer of the political scene and Auden the introvert; or, more specifically, we might say that the poetry reflects Auden's attitude toward and his adjustment to a too-slowly changing society, and his attempts at a solution of his own psychical problem. But these classifications present an obvious danger. Since his poetry expresses moods rather than the results of hard thought, the ideas in some of his early poems differ from those in some of his later ones on the same subject. A change—not a development, but the result of greater experience—is particularly evident, I think, in his attitude toward his personal problem. But too minute a breaking up of the subject matter is often neither possible nor feasible. The poems in which various aspects of his ideology are closely bound together are, in fact, numerous enough to make generalizations dangerous. In one poem the political background lends significance to his personal experience; in another the personal experience heightens the efficacy of his political castigations. 'Here on the cropped grass' is such a poem; and, although dealing with the post-depression era instead of the era of depression, his usual background, it well illustrates the close fusion of the two phases of his subject matter. Everywhere about him—in palace, movie, or cathedral—he hears the 'high thin rare continuous worship of the self-absorbed.' The people, as those in every age, have been, are being, and will continue to be duped. They are ignorant of the truth. Witness, for example, their attitude toward another war, pertinent at the present time. War is not necessary; it is not noble; it results from a lack of discipline; and those who die are not tragic. The pity is that the post-war generation has not learned the lesson that those fallen in the war would teach—

And out of the turf the bones of those fallen in war continue;
'Know then, cousin, the major cause of our collapse
Was a distortion in the human plastic by luxury produced,

Never higher than in our time were the vital advantages;
To matter entire, to the unbounded vigours of the instrument,
To all logical precision we were the rejoicing heirs.

But pompous, we assumed their power to be our own,
Believed machines to be our hearts' spontaneous fruit,
Taking our premises as shoppers take a tram.

While the disciplined love which alone could have employed these engines

Seemed far too difficult and dull, and when hatred promised
An immediate dividend, all of us hated.

Denying the liberty we knew quite well to be our destiny,
It dogged our steps with its accusing shadow
Until in every landscape we saw murder ambushed.

Unable to endure ourselves, we sought relief
In the insouciance of the soldier, the heroic sexual pose
Playing at fathers to impress the little ladies,

Call us not tragic; falseness made farcical our death:
Nor brave; ours was the will of the insane to suffer
By which since we could not live we gladly died:
And now we have gone for ever to our foolish graves.'

The theme of the necessity of discipline—inspired by Owen's
'The poetry is in the pity' and Kathy's 'To be rooted in life,
that's what I want,' and differing from some of the poet's
earlier themes and from his own practices—evoke moods that

> . . . give no permission to be idle
> For men are changed by what they do;
> And through loss and anger the hands of the unlucky
>   Love one another.

Visible everywhere are the signs of an industrial ruin brought
about by foreign competition; and yet little is done about it.
Those who should be exerting every nerve to remedy the
situation fritter away their time idly, deluding themselves,
attaching undue importance to family, themselves the victims
of a wrongly-emphasized education ('On Sunday Walks'). The
young intellectuals have likewise been guilty of this evasion.
They have squandered their time idly, have not faced reality,
and are unaware of the changes that have occurred in England.
In 'Get there if you can' Mr Auden warns them:

Shut up talking, charming in the best suits to be had in town,
Lecturing on navigation while the ship is going down.

Drop those priggish ways for ever, stop behaving like a
stone:
Throw the bath-chairs right away, and learn to leave ourselves alone.

If we really want to live, we'd better start at once to try;
If we don't, it doesn't matter, but we'd better start to die.

The employers, too, have changed for the worse. Despite a
restricted vision, they formerly had a love which expressed
itself through an ambitious zeal for personal glory—

The liberal appetite and power,
The rightness of a god.

To-day, however, they have engaged in guilty acts, have lost
nobility, individuality, and honour ('Our hunting fathers told
the story'). The land is, in fact, as barren as the country
envisaged by Mr Eliot in *The Waste Land*: the ruling classes are
restless; the heretofore submerged classes are even more so.
This age is to others not a Golden or a Silver Age, but an Age
of Ice, of spiritual barrenness.

No happiness through escape is possible. As the poet
stresses in 'Hearing of harvests rotting in the valleys,' each
'island' of refuge in turn loses its appeal, and the discontented
inhabitants move ever on to new 'islands.' Far better would it
be were we to remain on the spot 'and . . . rebuild our cities,
not dream of islands.' A healthy stock-taking is in order, because outwardly it would seem that in the poet's generation
history had 'struck a bad patch.'

What, then, must be the nature of this stock-taking? First,
we must do something about the distressed areas. This is a
difficult task, because those who stand to lose the most from
their ignorance of conditions know the least. The proletariat

are resigned to their pitiable lot ('Who will endure'); the upper classes will do nothing to remedy the conditions; the politicians are little better than boys—they have 'not contributed, but have diluted' ('Roar Gloucestershire, do yourself proud'); help must and will come from another source when the enemies of the free life—the curate, the club pro, the army man, etc., survivors of long-established institutions full of inherent weaknesses—fall, and from the wreckage emerges a new and finer life. Nor will average youths effect the change, because they are 'most of them dummies.' It must be the unusual youths who have not as yet become too closely linked with tradition, and can 'sheer off from old like gull from granite' ('Under boughs between our tentative endearments'). They must not, for example, let themselves be deluded into thinking that the man with beautiful manners, apparently master of the situation, is really free ('Watch any day his nonchalant pauses'); because he is not. He has merely taught himself how to maintain his poise in the presence of imminent disaster. It is true that one should lend a helping hand to the man afflicted with the missionary spirit ('Doom is dark and deeper than sea dingle'); but one must do more than be his friend, or the friend of the undeveloped, or of old ladies. A life of activity is necessary, even though it be barren of honour ('Will you turn a deaf ear').

From birth to death man is harassed by distractions, desires, mistakes, and inconsequential things to the extent that in important things he 'makes random answer to the crucial test.' He achieves neither graciousness nor thorough knowledge ('Between attention and attention'). Particularly is this true of youth. In 'Walk on air, do we?' the poet appeals to the 'heart of the heartless world' to make youth aware of the eternal needs, even if it is necessary to shock them into action; not to be fearers dreading harm, but men of courage at peace.

Because the various social groups are greatly at odds, a violent clash is inevitable. In fact, the clash will occur when a leader arises who can weld into one the diverse units desiring change. Then it will be too late for the financier, the college don, the clerics of the cathedrals, sports addicts, and others who have refused to recognize the growing unrest. Will the poet, because of his universal sympathy, have the power to avert the impending catastrophe? Will he be able to restore a normal, healthy order? Mr Auden is sufficiently an idealist to think that he will. With the aid of his friends he will create a new society in which life will be better than under the decayed ruins of the present order. It will be society's last change; and when those who have brought it about have grown old they will study their own comments on this changed and still changing order,

> Saying Aias
> To less and less,

temporarily forgetting what a poor thing is man ('What siren zooming').

The disillusioning thing about the struggle for those changes which will mean permanent improvement is the inability of mankind in general to pursue an ideal after some immediate needs have been satisfied. Some become discouraged from the lack of cohesion among those striving for a new order, as a result of which the capitalists can easily dominate them ('Control of the passes was, he saw, the key'); others lose interest because the world is incredulous of their warnings, and because there is no immediate practicability to their schemes; and still others lose interest because they have received cries of opprobrium instead of receiving praise for their attempts at living up to their ideals of truth and for their refusal to follow traditional paths ('By landscape reminded once').

In spite of the disaffection of would-be allies the poet never, even momentarily, loses his integrity. Through love he has arrived not only at a knowledge of himself, but of the con-

ditions in the world before which it is impossible to be passive
('May with its light behaving'). As he suggests to Isherwood
when reviewing their lives ('August for the people and their
favourite islands') the latter should devote the services of his
pen to bettering conditions, because the time is past when they
can live away from an upset world—

> The close-set eyes of mother's boy
> Saw nothing to be done; we look again:
> See Scandal praying with her sharp knees up,
> And Virtue stood at Weeping Cross,
> The green thumb to the ledger knuckled down,
> And Courage to his leaking ship appointed,
> Slim Truth dismissed without a character,
> And gaga Falsehood highly recommended.
>
> Greed showing shamelessly her naked money,
> And all Love's wondering eloquence debased
> To a collector's slang, Smartness in furs,
> And Beauty scratching miserably for food,
> Honour self-sacrificed for Calculation,
> And Reason stoned by Mediocrity,
> Freedom by Power shockingly maltreated,
> And Justice exiled till Saint Geoffrey's Day.

The way has been prepared for them by such men as Nansen,
Schweitzer, Freud, Groddeck, Lawrence ('revealed the sensations hidden by shame'), Kafka (recorded 'the sense of guilt')
and Proust ('on the self regard') ('Certainly our city').

As the poet tried to tell a young friend of unadventurous
temperament who would accept conditions as they are as less
dangerous than the attempt at altering them, all civilizations
die and those who refuse to recognize the new conditions are
the ones who suffer :

> Their fate must always be the same as yours,
> To suffer loss they were afraid of, yes,

Holders of one position, wrong for years.
                ('Since you are going to begin to-day')

And as he told the workers themselves: they submit to the daily drudgery for fear of getting the 'sack'; but their fears are 'fake' and can be dispelled. The day has passed when the workers are not important in the eyes of the world. Many ranks—including the mystic and scholar—have tried to console them, although really on the side of things as they are. But pay no attention to them ('Brothers, who when the sirens roar').

Thus reduced to the bare outlines of the 'thing said' it is obvious that the importance of Mr Auden's message does not lie in any practical programme of reform. The thought results from a sensitive person's impact with a reality which, because of a defective social and educational system, he never dreamed existed.[1] Fortunately, however, Mr Auden says much more than the foregoing summary suggests. In the work in which his poetic sensibility is most clearly revealed, his communication of these ideas is sufficiently powerful to stimulate in the reader a corresponding enthusiasm, awakening him to the problem to be solved. The means by which he does it is the subject of a later section of this essay.

II

When we turn from the political to the personal theme in Mr Auden's poetry—the theme which inspires many of his finest lyrics —we must not let our critical judgment be disturbed by the prominence of an unconventional (the homosexual) theme. With an honesty akin to that of Gide's in *Si le grain ne meurt*, Mr Auden has recorded the history of his attempt at reaching a satisfactory emotional adjustment. I say attempt because his latest work would indicate that he has not

[1]In Mr Day Lewis's novel *Starting Point* it was the General Strike of 1926 that afforded the opportunity for this impact. Anthony's political ideology in that novel does not differ widely from that of Day Lewis, Spender and Auden.

yet succeeded. Aware of the anomalous position of the Urning in modern society he has sought by his frankness of utterance to rid himself of any guilt or inferiority. The educational system, he says in *The Orators*, is partly to blame for the many wrong types of lovers: excessive lovers of self (the shy recluse), excessive lovers of their neighbours (those who live on their nerves), defective lovers (those who have escaped from life), and the perverted lovers (those who have lost their nerve and suffer every injustice). In a later section of this work he is less general, and by the mention of one specific ability of each he vivifies the many diverse types found in present-day civilization. He gives point to this catalogue by his 'summon': 'And there passed such cursing his father, and the curse was given him.' From a statement of the general he passes to a statement about himself. The 'Letter to a Wound' (*The Orators*) details his gradual absorption in his 'wound,' the suffering from which increased his sensibility and broadened his sympathy toward an understanding of others. Who, he asks, in a moment of introspection, are our real ancestors? 'The true ancestral line,' he says, 'is not necessarily a straight or continuous one'; his own true ancestor was his uncle, the homosexual.

Just as he is at pains to show that the ancestral line is not necessarily straight or continuous, so, too, does he rationalize his actions: the 'blood' wishes, even at the cost of regret, to travel further than that of his parent. Fully aware of the attempts being made by psychologists to solve certain problems of human behaviour—

> And cameras at the growing wood
> Are pointed; for the long lost good—
> > ('Now from my window-sill')

the poet warns them against over-hastiness in their attempts at a cure. Because even though he and his fellows are 'sick,' in order to escape their probings they will act under cover ['the mole's device'], be proud ['the carriage of peacock'], and put on a brave and insolent front ['rat's desperate courage'].[1] On the other hand, we must not think the state of the 'sick' an enviable one. (The poems themselves reveal that it is not.) The poet certainly wishes for his students a normal life where they will not 'have health and skill and beauty on the brain.' In 'The Chimneys are smoking' the poet goes one step further and makes an indirect plea for the day when the homosexual will be recognized by society, so that he—the 'left-handed' ('Fleeing the short-haired mad executives')—need feel no shame. The poem is intensely personal and deeply moving, revealing the characteristics mentioned in 'Now from my window-sill':

> And since our desire cannot take that route which is straight-
> est
> Let us choose the crooked, so implicating these acres,
> These millions in whom already the wish to be one
>
> > Like a burglar is stealthily moving,
> > That these, on the new façade of a bank
> > Employed, or conferring at health resort,
> > May, by circumstance linked,
> > More clearly act our thought.

With conditions as they are, it is useless to expect from the ordinary biography anything but superficial facts, and even those facts are worthless because a sympathetic and understanding interpretation of them is lacking. 'It was Easter as I walked in the public gardens' and 'A shilling life will give you

[1] The 'brave and insolent front' is noticeable in *Letters from Iceland*. At times in this volume the poet seems to seek desperately to cover beneath a cloak of studied smartness and sheer bravado a sense of guilt forced upon him by the *mores* of society. The aspect of his personality here revealed is definitely less pleasant than those aspects revealed in his other volumes. Except as a further indication of Mr Auden's prosodic skill I do not think *Letters from Iceland* will add anything to his stature. Instead of shocking the reader, as I think he hopes to do, he succeeds only in arousing his pity that so much energy has been spent in doing something so little worthy of his talents. The book gives every indication of being nothing more than the fulfilment of a contract with the publishers. But *Spain*, a poem which lifts Mr Auden out of himself, possesses the finest qualities of his genius.

all the facts' are important approaches to Mr Auden's poetry
because of the statement in the former and implication in the
latter that only for a time can the unorthodox be forced into
'conformity with the orthodox bone, with organized fear, the
articulated skeleton.'

As one grows older, maintains the poet in 'Now the leaves
are falling fast,' the chances for happiness in love are fewer,
and even those are impossible because of the censure of
'whispering neighbours'—

> And the nightingale is dumb,
> And the angel will not come.

Even from those who try to understand comes only such misunderstanding as tempts him to ask

> Were they or he
> The physician, bridegroom and incendiary?
>> ('Just as his dream foretold')

Love, after all, is an individual problem which each person
must solve for himself. For Mr Auden it is a form of escape
from the insecurity of a troubled world:

> So, insecure, he loves and love
> Is insecure, gives less than he expects.
> He knows not if it be seed time to display
> Luxuriantly in a wonderful fructification
> Or whether it be but a degenerate remnant
> Of something immense in the past but now
> Surviving only as the infectiousness of disease
> Or in the malicious caricature of drunkenness;
> Its end glossed over by the careless but known long
> To finer perception of the mad and ill.
>> ('It was Easter as I walked')

As John Nower said in 'Paid on Both Sides': 'We cannot tell
where we shall find it, though we all look for it till we do; and

what others tell us is no use to us.' It cannot be defined by negation ('Love by ambition'), although it is first released through a kiss ('Sentries against inner and outer'), and it is seldom successful except in stories ('The silly fool').

Numerous selections from *Poems* and *Look, Stranger!* reveal with amazing candour episodes in the love-life of an Urning. 'From the very first coming down' depicts the end to a love after a year had passed and 'love's worn circuit' had 're-begun.' The poet, while awaiting in the country the arrival of the beloved receives a letter expressing the beloved's inability to join him. Realizing that one of them has changed, he accepts the end—

> I, decent with the seasons, move
> Different or with a different love.

'It's no use raising a shout' is a variation on a similar situation. The end has come; nothing remains to do except to face their problem:

> A bird used to visit this shore:
> It isn't going to come any more.
> I've come a very long way to prove
> No land, no water, and no love.

That the beloved might not be too honourable is suggested in 'What's in your mind.' The poet muses on the thoughts of the beloved at his side—is he thinking of love? of money? of stealing? Whatever it is, however, let him not try to fool him by going through the gestures of love; rather, 'strike for the heart, and have' him there. Nor was constancy the poet's great virtue! The theme of 'Before this loved one,' reveals that there had been other relationships before the present one; and the gratitude of the new love toward him was not only less to him than the loss of the old, but anything that happened between them would only intensify his feelings about the old love.

As a means of self-justification the poet poses a certain

question: first, in 'To ask the hard question' and more clearly in 'Fish in the unruffled lakes.' Why, he asks, is man afraid to remember that by absence of conscience, by surrender to natural desires, and by lack of conception of duty the birds, beasts, and fish find freedom, whereas man

> For atonement or for luck;
> We must love our loves,
> On each beast and bird that moves
> Turn an envious look.

It is clear from Mr Auden's poetry that with greater experience the moods in which he realizes the necessity for a certain stabilization of his emotional life have become more frequent. Many love-lyrics in *Look, Stranger!* have lost the pert smartness of some of the earlier poems on the same theme. These later lyrics possess a passionate intensity and beauty of diction that give them abiding worth. What is not clear, however—and it is driven home in 'Dear, though the night is gone'—is the poet's willingness to follow in his private life the regimen of discipline he knows to be necessary.

The theme of 'The earth turns over,' one of many poems stressing the awareness of one person of another, would be impossible in a heterosexual relationship. It possesses genuine passion. The poet realizes that any attempt on his part to forward the matter brings failure. Only by drifting might it develop:

> Lost if I steer. Gale of desire may blow
> Sailor and ship past the illusive reef,
> And I yet land to celebrate with you
> Birth of a natural order and of love;
> With you enjoy the untransfigured scene,
> My father down the garden in his gaiters,
> My mother at her bureau writing letters,
> Free to our favours, all our titles gone.

'To lie flat on the back' and 'That night when joy began' stress a similar emotion. In each, the relationship begins nervously and as an episode; with consummation, however, it develops into love and steadfastness. 'Let the florid music praise' is metaphysical, explaining the power of the beloved's look to thwart any attempt against him on the part of the lover 'unloved.'

Every person in love derives a certain illusion of power from his state; he not only possesses a greater sense of being freed from himself and his surroundings, but also feels that only then is life really full of meaning. And yet, in spite of this feeling, love is not enough to meet 'the flood on which all move and wish to move' ('Love had him fast'). In 'Easily, my dear, you move' the poet, addressing the beloved in a vein of high purpose, expresses with even more positiveness the idea that, inspired by love, the lover can accomplish great things of every sort. Repeatedly, Mr Auden calls attention to one phase of love; the lover loving but unloved, summarizing in 'Night covers up the rigid land' much of the story:

> For each love to its aim is true,
> And all kinds seek their own;
> You love your life and I love you,
> So I must lie alone.

III

From the foregoing exposition certain conclusions can be drawn about the subject matter of Mr Auden's poetry. He is not a thinker in the sense that he has developed a system or a philosophy of his own. His sympathies and interests are definitely Leftist-Labour. The good he can do the cause does not, however, lie in any positive programme of action. He sees conditions that cry aloud the necessity for change, and he can make us see them. A dozen 'leaders' on conditions in the 'distressed areas' are not as effective as one of his better poems on the same subject. He makes an impassioned plea for tolerance toward the Urning whose position in society is anomalous even though he is the product of that society. If he tends to alienate that sympathy by some passages in *Letters from Iceland*, we must remember they reflect but one mood of the chameleon-like character of Mr Auden, an adept at presenting his own innumerable moods be they of tenderness, disillusionment, generosity, satire, defiance, inferiority, tolerance, depression because of injustice, or hopefulness.

IV

But what of the tools by which the poet communicates these moods? And what of the scene against which he sets his characters?

Mr Auden frankly likes landscapes in which are visible abandoned mine shafts, tumbling factories, and general signs of decay. He also likes high places. It is interesting, in fact, to recall the many poems that reveal him musing on the state of the world from a scar, a hill, a cliff, or an upper room, all frequently at the edge of the sea. The title poem of *Look, Stranger!* reveals the many qualities of his descriptive powers. Without Wordsworth's tendency toward moralization, he possesses his ability of evoking a scene by a few carefully chosen details :

> Look, stranger, at this island now
> The leaping light for your delight discovers,
> Stand stable here
> And silent be,
> And through the channels of the ear
> May wander like a river
> The swaying sound of the sea
>
> Here at the small field's ending pause
> Where the chalk wall falls to the foam, and its tall ledges

Oppose the pluck
And knock of the tide,
And the shingle scrambles after the suck-
ing surf, and the gull lodges
A moment on its sheer side.

Far off like floating seeds the ships
Diverge on urgent voluntary errands;
And the full view
Indeed may enter
And move in memory as now these clouds do,
That pass the harbour mirror
And all the summer through the water saunter.

Natural forces, frequently sentient, help to reveal the poet's
mood and to key the poem:

. . . you may hear the wind
Arriving driven from the ignorant sea
To hurt itself on pane, on bark of elm
Where sap unbaffled rises, being spring. . .
('Who stands, the crux left of the watershed')

And on a different spring day he

. . . walked in the public gardens
Hearing the frogs exhaling from the pond,
Watching traffic of magnificent cloud
Moving without anxiety on open sky—
('It was Easter as I walked')

With Debussy-like impressionism in a description of lunar
beauty he communicates his own harmonizing mood:

This like a dream
Keeps other time
And daytime is
The loss of this;

For time is inches
And the heart's changes
Where ghost has haunted
Lost and wanted

('This lunar beauty')

The first two stanzas of 'Now from my window-sill' paint another spring night. The clarity of detail reflects the poet's introspective mood of regret at his own psychical state.

Like those of Spender and Day Lewis, Mr Auden's figures are fresh, contemporary, and frequently biting. Cathedrals, for example, are

Luxury liners laden with souls,
Holding to the east their hulls of stone,
The high thin rare continuous worship
Of the self-absorbed;

('Here on the cropped grass')

and an ironic note appears in such a verse as 'Climbing with you was easy as a vow' ('Fleeing the short-haired mad executive'). Mr Auden's greatest achievement is, however, his remarkable ability in communicating all aspects of different emotional experiences by the perfect suitability of his prosodic form. Whether grave or gay, tender or bitter, idealistic or disillusioned, one realizes that the clothing of his thought, particularly in his later work, is the right clothing. In order to achieve this he makes extensive use of half-rhymes like lean-alone, hall-hill, strain-stone, tipped-topped. These occur in couplets (e.g. the choruses in *Paid on Both Sides*); in alternating half-rhymes, as in 'To lie flat on the back,' (really a new form of sonnet); in quatrains; and in numerous other combinations, even internally, as in 'Epilogue':

'O where are you going?' said reader to rider,
'That valley is fatal when furnaces burn,
Yonder's the midden whose odours will madden,
That gap is the grave where the tall return';

The quatrain is put to effective use in a poem depicting a love which having begun nervously and as a thing of the moment developed into steadfastness:

> That night when joy began
> Our narrowest veins to flush
> We waited for the flash
> Of morning's levelled gun.
>
> ('That night when joy began ')

The inherent sadness of those who flock to the casinos to gamble is admirably caught in 'Casino':

> But here no nymph comes naked to the youngest shepherd,
> The fountain is deserted, the laurel will not grow;
> The labyrinth is safe but endless, and broken
> Is Ariadne's thread.

The short fourth line reflects the flatness, the hopelessness of the protagonists' lives. In 'Easily, my dear, you move' the short sixth line of the stanza slows down the entire stanza, increasing the vein of high purpose, tenderness, and even of ecstasy. The same stanza is otherwise interesting in that instead of a uniform syllabic structure the verses vary from nine to twelve syllables, but the rhythm remains regularly four stressed:

> Shall idleness ring then your eyes like the pest?
> O will you unnoticed and mildly like the rest,
> Will you join the lost in their sneering circles,
> Forfeit the beautiful interest and fall
> Where the engaging face in the face of the betrayer,
> And the pang is all?

Mr Auden utilizes repetition and the turn with admirable results. In 'Look there! The sunk road winding,' he communicates to us the unfortunate generation:

> In legend all were simple,
> And held the straitened spot;
> But we in legend not,
> Are not simple.

Again the short fourth verse gives a decided sense of fall, of lack of idealism. He uses repetition, too, for sketching a satiric portrait of a man who sacrificed his dreams to material success. The short verses intensify the irony, and his use in the last stanza of 'spacious' to describe days that were the opposite heightens the ironic effect ('As it is, plenty').

It is natural that anyone as much interested in Norse poetry and the older literature as Mr Auden avowedly is should use alliteration[1]; and he uses it frequently, as in the already referred to 'Here on the cropped grass':

> A fathom of earth, alive in air,
> Aloof as an admiral on the old rocks.

The effect of the sagas is more clearly revealed in his at times cryptic concentration, and in the imagery portraying a racial subconsciousness. Ballads, also, have exerted an influence, particularly in his satiric work. Both in poems and plays short, crisp, dry verses intensify the mood of a narrowed horizon. They also communicate the breathless rush and worry of the thought. 'O what a sound' satisfies all the conditions of a typical ballad; almost similar in construction, in fact, to the famous 'Edward.'

'It's no use raising a shout,' with its origin in the popular song, enhances the utter commonplaceness of the situation.[2]

---

[1] Other influences may of course be responsible for his use of alliteration, a device which has never been absent from English poetry. The revival of interest in *Piers Plowman* may be one; and an even more powerful one is the poetry of Gerard Manley Hopkins.

[2] Further interesting metrical experiments may be found in 'We have brought you' (from the 'Journal of an Airman'), 'There are some birds in these valleys' (*Poems*, p. 143), 'Watching in three planes,' 'Brothers, who when the sirens roar,' 'Out on the lawn I lie in bed,' and 'O for doors to be open,' with its refrain:

> Cried the cripples to the silent statue,
> The six beggared cripples.

Mr Auden's use of rime royal in his 'Letter to Byron' captures much of the spirit of the addressee's *Don Juan*, although it is generally thinner than the original.[1] *Spain* is one of his most distinguished prosodic achievements. The use of the refrain 'But to-day the struggle' heightens and gives point to the picture of a past, a present, and a future Spain.

But I would not have the reader think that Mr Auden is at all times equally successful. In innumerable instances the form not only adds nothing to the thought, but actually robs the idea of its force by riveting the attention on the chaotic and strange dress rather than on the idea. In other words, the form dissipates rather than concentrates the effect of the idea, and by so doing removes the experiment from the sphere of poetry.

There is little question in my mind but that Mr Auden is the foremost of the younger group of poets. He has done much to quicken our senses toward two groups—the workers and the Urnings, and to point out where many of the evils of contemporary civilization lie. But one fear constantly forces itself to the surface—the fear that a lack of discipline will eventually exact a toll from the quality of their work. Both have learned from experience that for any abiding satisfaction a rigid discipline is necessary; but they seem reluctant to practise it. They should remember that the highest poetry is not a direct outpouring of passion, but a sublimation.

Mr Auden's ideas are not so important as the way in which he expresses them. In his early work he is frequently obscure, not only because of the presence of private jokes which only a

---

[1] I have said nothing of the subject matter of *The Dog Beneath the Skin*, *The Ascent of F6*, *On the Frontier*, or *Letters from Iceland*. The poetry in these volumes has none of the obscurity of *Poems* or *Look, Stranger!* In fact, it has a crystalline clarity. It is incisive, frequently genuinely funny, and often most cuttingly satiric. But in the first three it is impossible to separate Auden's from Isherwood's contribution, and I have already expressed my opinion of *Letters from Iceland*. A reading of Mr Isherwood's *Mr Norris Changes Trains* throws some light on the possible characteristics of his contributions to the plays. If Mr Auden has written the poetry, it is Mr Isherwood who has furnished many of the ideas of surprising pungency.

few intimates may understand, but because he oversimplifies the communication of complex experiences. He has used the imagery of psychoanalysis for the illumination of the sub-conscious mind and has left the uninitiated bewildered. In *Look, Stranger!*, he has expressed himself in an idiom which is clear, forceful, imaginative, and at times deeply moving.

It is, of course, still too early to prophesy Mr Auden's ultimate position. Much that he has so far published will be forgotten, and rightly so. But there can be no doubt that the corpus of his good work, already large enough to merit serious attention, communicates the truth as he has seen it. Whether or not the communication of this truth is sufficiently universal to interest another age is the concern of that age.

STEPHEN SPENDER

MR STEPHEN SPENDER, having several times expressed his views on the proper subject matter for poets, has sought in his own poetry to put his theories into practice. Aware that at the present time many things in the world are worth writing about, it is to him a sign of decadence when poets or novelists concern themselves with autobiographical themes. His poetry attempts to deal with the political subject in the larger meaning of the term—man's relation to society.

Tendencies *per se* hold no interest for him because art, he maintains, is not concerned with the illustration of any point of view. It presents its subject in a new form and the observation which inspires the subject must of necessity be external and real. The poet, however much he might desire justice, must not be concerned with himself. It is his duty to bring into being a world quite external to his own interests; just as in a poem, he must not shove himself into it.

The result is, however, almost pure autobiography. He maintains that 'pleasure or sorrow in the incidents of life cut off from all theorizing or opinion are the sources of lyricism.' Not only must poets first feel whatever they make others feel to any marked degree, but (to quote Hazlitt) 'they must have this feeling all their lives. It is not a fashion got up and put on for the occasion; it is the very condition and ground-work of their being.' The value of Mr Spender's poetry lies in the force of its communication of the reactions of a sensitive person to the unsettled world conditions of to-day. Although autobiographical, it is not narrowly egocentric. Objective though he attempts to be, subjectivity is the result.

Mr Spender's own dissatisfaction with the society in which he is living has thwarted the normal outlet for those general emotions which we classify as love. As a result, imperfect though it be at times, Mr Spender has made an architecture of his own poetry which exists by reference to his reaction to the industrial towns and the distresse adreas. One must not, however, let the new manner of his presentation delude him into thinking that his poetry is primarily cerebral. It is passionate and emotional; it is the poetry of feeling—feeling, however, which in his good work is carefully controlled.

Contrary to the beliefs of many regarding the present age, there is undoubtedly a greater element of innocence in society to-day than has existed for several generations. This innocence makes frankness possible. That which Mr Spender believes has been denied to Henry James—the freedom to write of lovers—is possible to him. Love is the dominant theme of his poetry.

Similar though the subject matter of many of the poems seems to be, analysis reveals that no two communications of his experience cover the same ground. The poems comprise a diorama of a sensitive person's contacts with the world. The architectonic quality of Mr Spender's poetry is most evident in those poems dealing with love. Urningism interests him. He not only sees traces of it in *The Pupil* of Henry James, but in his excellent appraisal of W. H. Auden he discusses the possible use or purpose of the Urning in modern society, because more than any other person he possesses irresponsibility. He recognizes, however, the danger of too great an engrossment in the personal problem. And he realizes that abnormality is not, as some foolishly believe, a guarantee of superior powers.

Having read Freud, Mr Spender accepts certain of his tenets as the cause of one of the pertinent problems of contemporary society. The poems 'My parents quarrel in the neighbour room' and 'My parents kept me from children who were rough' and the passage in the last section of *Vienna* beginning 'It surely was my father' suggest the possible reason for the protagonist's psychical state. Apart from the foregoing three passages, Mr Spender makes no apologia for that state. He accepts it; one might almost say he accepts it as the norm. Certainly there is no trace of morbidity in his presentation.

An examination of the poems reveals the several aspects of Mr Spender's treatment of personal love. 'Not to you I sighed' and 'Acts passed beyond the boundary of mere wishing,' two poems revealing a delicate sensitivity usually thought of as feminine in quality, but one which is, unfortunately, almost purely masculine, portray the gradual awakening of love.

Love brings fulfilment, it is true, but with it also comes the torture of jealousy. But what is even more important is that love, or at least the illusion of love, can be shattered by some inconsequential thing. Mr Spender communicates this in three poems, 'Never being, but always at the edge of Being,' 'After success, your little afternoon success,' and 'Alas, when he laughs it is not he.' Unrequited love will warp the character and ambition will be an effective instrument in preventing love. Such is the theme of 'Shapes of death haunt life.' Life rather should be simply the act of living and enjoying. The unfortunate thing, however, is that at the moment the lover is achieving fulfilment, he can harm the beloved so that ever after 'his hand will show error.' 'Your body is stars whose million glitter here' and 'For T. A. R. H.' round out Spender's attitude toward love by communicating its transforming power and the despair which almost naturally follows. It can easily be deduced from the foregoing that what is new and unusual in the subject matter of his treatment of love is his honesty in presenting the various phases, good as well as unfortunate, in the emotional life of an Urning.

In the final section of *The Still Centre* he develops with an even greater intensity than ever before, this fettering aspect of his personality. He remains determined to express the truth as he sees it, at the same time conscious that there might be a greater truth than that experienced by him. In order to arrive at that truth he is willing to subject himself to a thorough self-probing and to abide by the results. The most passionate poems in his latest volume, like those in the earlier ones, are those in which he treats homo-sexuality as the norm for him. Yet in his determination to be honest he can rid himself neither of a sense of inferiority nor of a sense of guilt. He realizes in 'The Human Situation' that he must be as he is—a series of contradictions, but the sum total of numerous influences on his own and on his parents' lives. His way of life is not easy, but it is the only possible one for him. 'Darkness and Light,' 'The Mask,' and 'Variations on My Life' further illumine his personal problem which he outwardly resolves in 'The Separation,' 'The Room Above the Square,' and other love lyrics in the volume.

The most outstanding quality pervading his poetry, if not the most novel, is the spiritualization and the expansion of the feelings connected with the personal problem into the love which embraces the suffering and the unfortunate—a Whitmanesque quality which Lawrence would have deplored, and which unfortunately was sometimes jolted by their ordinariness.

II

Much of the love which Mr Spender had for his fellows is the direct outgrowth of pity. It is here that the political aspect of his poetry is most evident. The contrast of the 'pale lily boys' who 'flaunt their bright lips' for money in the port with the worldly ship owner; the men standing idly at the corner of the street unable to find work; the workers who are prisoners of the machine; the starving unfortunates, the victims of the war, the boom, and the depression all evoke his pity. He makes no attempt to see them through rosy glasses or to present them in such form to his readers. The problem is, of course, so to remedy economic conditions that such things can no longer exist. Mr Spender is poet enough not to put forward any definite Utopian scheme as a panacea for existing ills. His contribution lies in the fact that, possessed with the sensibility of a true poet, he experiences more acutely than does the average man the hopeless welter of present-day chaos. His contribution lies in his ability to communicate to the reader the intensity of his own reactions. Those readers who complain that Mr Spender lacks a definite ideology fail to understand his avowed purpose—the purpose of genuine poetry.

I have suggested the importance of pity in Mr Spender's work. Pity is the keynote of Wilfred Owen's poetry and of his influence on Mr Spender. He has revealed to a brother artist its possible use in poetry. In Owen's case it was the pity of war; in Mr Spender's, the pity toward the victims of the postwar conditions.

Pity is the germ of 'The Prisoner':

> My pity moves amongst them like a breeze
> On walls of stone
> Fretting for summer leaves, or like a tune
> On ears of stone.

And aware that at no time in their lives have they been free, that from the very time of their birth they were doomed to the 'airs that choke,' he concludes:

> No, no, no,
> It is too late for anger,
> Nothing prevails
> But pity for the grief they cannot feel.

Pity, too, is his attitude toward the young men in *Vienna* who, finding themselves in the chaos resulting from war, have not sent firm roots into a soil so similar to the barren rockiness of T. S. Eliot's 'The Waste Land.' Says Mr Spender of these young men:

We can read their bodies like advertisements
On hoardings, shouting with common answers.
Not saying, life is happy, unhappy is ill,
Death is reward, law just, but only
Life is life, body is body, a day
Is the sun: there is left only beauty
Of merest being, of swimming, of somehow not starving:
And merest beauty has a sun-tanned body
Available for uses, but only sold. Pathic
Strength of marble thighs, Greek chest, a torso
Without purposive veins travelling to hands.

In spite of the fact that these young men 'have spilled and bled' his 'veins of trust across their sport,' in spite of the fact that they have been wholly selfish in their attitude toward him, he realizes that the love in him, which is almost an universal love, prevents him from assuming an unforgiving attitude. It is not only pity for them, it is greater than pity—it is love. He says:

There is no question more of not forgiving
Forgiveness become my only feeling
To understand their lack of understanding
Has absorbed my entire loving,
Yet sometimes I wish that I were loud and angry
Without this human mind like a doomed sky
That loves, as it must enclose, all.

Important as was Owen's effect on his work, Mr Spender believes that the poet of to-day, no less than the poet of the future, is faced with a problem greater than that of Owen. He must be able to understand and communicate the complexities of the world that grows daily more complicated. This remains the peculiar duty of the poet rather than of the statesman or philosopher, because 'poetry is the only branch of knowledge that can form a synthesis of our experiences, so overwhelming,

so obscure and paralyzing.' The effecting of such a synthesis
will enable man to understand the soul of man.

But how can the synthesis be effected when even the poet is
confused and bewildered; when he is

> Without that once clear aim, the path of flight
> To follow for a life-time through white air,
> This century chokes me under roots of night
> I suffer like history in Dark Ages, where
> Truth lies in dungeons, from which drifts no whisper?

Love is necessary. The poem from which the foregoing selection is taken bears a close kinship to Keats' 'Ode to a Nightingale,' particularly in the poet's escape through poetry—'This
writing is my only wings away.'

III

I think it is true that no young poet of to-day, whether he
admits it or not, is wholly free from the influence of D. H.
Lawrence. Certainly he has been an important factor in Mr
Spender's poetry. From the point of view of subject matter he
has encouraged him through example to a courageous frankness of statement and an incisive clarity of observation.
Lawrence has been spoken of as the champion of Priapus as a
Messiah. In certain poems Mr Spender reveals himself an
ardent disciple of Lawrence. In 'oh young men, oh young
comrades' he admonishes the younger generation properly to
evaluate their physical attributes:

> . . . the fabulous possessions
> which begin with your body and your fiery soul;

and in 'Passing, men are sorry for birds in cages,' he apostro-
phizes physical delight.

Two passages which clearly reveal his lyrical quality deal
with this subject. In 'I think continually of those who were
truly great,' he says:

What is precious is never to forget
The essential delight of the blood drawn from ageless springs
Breaking through rocks in worlds before our earth.
Never to deny its pleasure in the morning simple light
Nor its grave evening demand for love.
Never to allow gradually the traffic to smother
With noise and fog the flowering of the spirit.

And in 'Not palaces, an era's crown,' he calls to the senses—

Eye, gazelle, delicate wanderer,
Drinker of the horizon's fluid line ;
Ear that suspends on a chord
The spirit drinking timelessness;
Touch, love, all senses:—

to leave their 'singing feasts,' to enter the world of strife, and
not to rest until conditions are so changed that all men will be
equal.

The most important effect, however, which Lawrence has
had on Mr Spender is the manner in which he has directed the
younger poet's attitude toward life. Mr Spender is frequently
spoken of as being a member of the growing group of English
Communists. His adherence to the Communist cause arises, I
think, from the fact that he believes with Lawrence that under
a new regime, life itself might have a chance. In Lawrence's
later poems, as well as in his letters, he hammers at the idea
that what the world most needs is an opportunity for life.
This, with its accomplishment by means of love, is the keynote of Mr Spender's poetry.

There is no hopelessness in his work, nor a surrender to
imponderable discouraging forces. At the very time, he says,
'when grief pours freezing over us,'

surely from hunger
We may strike fire, like fire from flint?
And our strength is now the strength of our bones

Clean and equal like the shine from snow
And the strength of famine and of our enforced idleness,
And it is the strength of our love for each other;

and he urges his comrades not to let the failures of banks, of
religion, or of government prevent them from revealing

. . . the Spring-like resources of the tiger
Or of plants who strike out new roots to gushing waters.

Indignation toward the apathetic masses so evident in many of
Lawrence's *Last Poems* is never evident in Mr Spender's work.

Mr Spender is, moreover, a better prosodist than Lawrence.
Because of this he communicates to us through his verse the
passion which Lawrence could only communicate through
conversation. His indignation against Dolfuss and his regime
does not have its basis in narrow political differences, but in the
larger meaning of the political question—the free flowering of
the spirit —the flowering which can take place only where
freedom is permitted. The pity which the sight of the Viennese
youth of his own generation evoked because they have been
denied a chance for life, leads to his indignation against a
government where such things are possible. It is obvious, I
think, that an analysis of the subject matter of Mr Spender's
poetry leads to but one possible conclusion. It is motivated by
his intense dissatisfaction with modern political institutions.

Anxious as Mr Spender seems to be for a revolution that
will bring to the masses a greater opportunity for a fuller life,
he at no time is blind to the problem confronting the artist.
There is little question but that he is on the side of the proletariat. Yet he carefully refrains from saying that the proletariat
is better than any other class. Artists must insist on human
values. If they do this consistently, and a need for a revolution
becomes apparent for these human values, that will make the
revolution. Youthful it is, to be sure, yet the passionate
protest compels the thoughtful reader to seek an answer to the

questions which Mr Spender poses. Something must be done,
but what? The poet having posed the question has done his
part. The solution is the problem for the rest of us.

But would a revolution be productive of progress? In fact, is
any progress being effected in the world? Mr Spender is at
times doubtful:

> only Perhaps. Can be that we grow smaller
> donnish and bony shut in our racing prison:
> headlines are walls that shake and close
> the dry dice rattled in their wooden box.
>
> Can be deception of things only changing. Out there
> perhaps growth of humanity above the plain
> hangs: not the timed explosion, oh but Time
> monstrous with stillness like the himalayan range.

The same passion for a new social order persists in *Trial of a
Judge* as in the earlier poems, and is continued in *The Still
Centre*. Except for a few poems such as 'An Elementary School
Class Room in a Slum' and 'Thought During an Air Raid' they
are disappointing because they are largely repetitions of earlier
statements.

IV

Too frequently a discussion of a poet overlooks the one
thing that lends importance to his subject matter: the manner
of his communication, on which will depend, of course, his
ultimate position as a poet. It is this very essence of his work
—'Not the thing said but the way of saying it'—that is most
difficult of appraisal by a contemporary. In fact, it is impossible
to pass with finality upon the poet's manner of communication. Tendencies in his work may, however, give some measure
of his achievement.

The youthfulness that is apparent in Mr Spender's attitude toward the world is not a characteristic of his prosody. It is true that he has not yet revealed the power for sustained flight. *Vienna*, for example, in spite of numerous passages of genuine poetic worth is uneven—perhaps, in the last analysis, a failure. Too frequently indignation has submerged the poet, and too often a lack of perspective is evident. Yet, prosodically, it shows an advance. No slavish imitation of Gerard Manley Hopkins can be cited, yet the rhythms of certain passages—the opening for example—more than suggest that Mr Spender has read the elder poet with profit. But imperfect as the poem is as a whole, if the reader is apathetic to the contemporary scene, it rouses him; if he is already awake to its problems, it heartens him.

His poetry is difficult because it is concentrated, not because his thinking is vague. The frequent absence of the definite article heightens the sense of compactness, and in so doing enhances the passionate quality of the verse. Mr Spender has experimented with equal success in numerous stanza forms. He is artist enough to suit the form to the subject matter; and, what is more important, to key his work to the right tone. If the subject matter is small the tone is conversational; if it rises to greater importance, so, too, does the tone. The tone constantly bolsters and gives greater significance to the idea than it would otherwise possess. That the reader is not conscious of the poet's technique until he tears the work apart in order to see the technique does great credit to the artist. When it is torn apart the magic disappears, only to reappear, however, the moment the poem is again read in its entirety. I speak, of course, of the best poems, none of which is probably great. *Vienna*, as I have already suggested, is a different matter.

For his first essay in the dramatic form, *Trial of a Judge*, Mr Spender, consciously or unconsciously, has unfortunately used Mr T. S. Eliot's *Murder in the Cathedral* as his model. Like his model, his play is deficient in characterization, in suspense, and in conflict—in short, in those qualities which for most of us are necessary for good drama; although it does contain a few moving and powerful scenes. The dialogue ranges from prose of the streets through that of the English ritual to poetry that surpasses any in the earlier work. The latter is reflective, impassioned, vivid, and above all, nostalgic from a sense of lost idealism. One will best appreciate its merits in the library where there is time leisurely to enjoy the many beautiful monodies of the Judge, of Petra's brother, of his fiancée, and of his mother. The play starts the suspicion, however, confirmed in *The Still Centre*, that the poet works in a limited range that tends toward monotony.

The strength of a poet lies in his imagination; in his ability to fix indelibly in the mind of the reader by the apt choice of epithet the picture not only of the exterior of the person being described, but also of the inmost recesses of his character and soul. He not only reveals the object, but everything around it. Mr Spender, with a freshness and vividness of characterization not unlike those of Lawrence, is able to combine the seemingly incongruous to form unforgettable images. Wit is everywhere present in his work. When he tells the young men that they must break away from the great houses where the ghosts of the past are prisoned—

those ladies like flies perfect in amber
those financiers like fossils of bones in coal—

he fixes indelibly on our minds the picture of an anachronistic society. More vivid of a vanishing era is his description of the proprietor of the Pension Beaurepas.

Winged tie. Winged nose. A bleared, active eye.
The stick and strut of a sprucer day.

The yellow sheet is the product of the newsmen who

. . . run like points of compass: their arms are
gusts that carry sheets of moldy paper:
our eyes mud those scraps rub on.

Mr Spender's antipathy to the Viennese Fascists is unmistakable in his description of Major Fey's 'strong,' white face as 'a
wet handkerchief shot through with two lead bullets.' In reading his description of the lost generation—the young men
who are devoid of any aim in life—we not only see them, but
we feel Mr Spender's tremendous pity because such situations
can exist.

Not only in the description of persons, however, is visible
Mr Spender's sensitive observation of the world. His images
are fresh and contemporary. Flags blown on a wintry day are
to him 'like whippets tugging.' The airplane gliding into the
aerodrome is like a moth—

> More beautiful and soft than any moth
> With burring furred antennae feeling its huge path
> Through dusk.

In the same poem, however, the description of the chimneys,
revealing a straining after effect, is less fortunate. Somewhat
forced, too, is the description of the pylons as

> . . those pillars
> Bare like nude, giant girls that have no secret.

We can, however, share the troubled experience of the poet
when he lay awake.

> . . . and the sea's distant fretless scansion
> By imagination scourged rose to a fight
> Like the town's roar, *pouring out apprehension*.

Strongly reminiscent of Lawrence is his description of the way
in which

> Hope and despair and the small vivid longings
> Like minnows gnaw the body;

and of the cries of evening

> . . . while the paw
> Of dark creeps up the turf.

Wit and the straining for surprise are the ingredients of the
simile of the broken pipe:

> That heavy-wrought briar with the great pine face
> Now split across like a boxer's hanging dream
> Of punishing a nigger . . .

Stronger, I think, are some of the figures from *Vienna*. The
simile of the blue sky—'Memory of sky as blue as woman's
veins'—flushes a train of thought. Trenchant irony motivates
the simile of the snipers:

> To pick men with a gun is delicate
> As pointing cleanest crochet.

How brief and ineffective are the spirits that 'flared up as a
match spurts!'

Frequently Mr Spender uses single epithets with telling
force. The word 'easy,' for example, in the following description of flowers stirs the imagination of the reader:

> We brought easy flowers in crude wreaths
> Daisies, nasturtium, corn flower, sorrel, dandelion.

Exact, too, is his portrayal of the stork's flight, as the 'wave-
winged ' storks.

In the later volumes the images more and more give the
impression of being consciously sought for; only rarely do
they possess the quality of inevitability. Mr Spender will not,
therefore, rank as an imagist of prime importance; nor does his
chief interest lie in that aspect of his work, pregnant though
many of them are. Nowhere has he surpassed the felicity of the
early 'Eye, gazelle, delicate wanderer.' Nor in spite of frequent
skilful use of repetition, as in the following, will he assume
great importance as a prosodist:

> Whether the man living or the man dying
> Whether this man's dead life, or that man's life
> dying

His real life a fading light, his real death a
light growing
The square windows of the prison square surround
him dumbly,

Ministerial lips smile, but what's transparent
As thin glass is their transparent smile
Over thin lips: the glass is dashed down suddenly
And murder glares.

His limited prosodic range noticeable in *Trial of a Judge*
becomes even more so in *The Still Centre*. Because he has not
sufficiently varied the music of his verse one cannot read much
of his work at one time, and, in spite of the diverse metrical
patterns he calls into use, the effect in his later work is not as
varied as in his earlier. He achieves an elegiac quality that tends
to pall. One longs in vain for more poems with the energy of
'What I expected.'

But the chief interest of Mr Spender does not depend on
isolated images or on a wide musical and emotional range. It is
heartening in a seemingly apathetic age, when only those
whose roots are firmly lodged in a pre-war soil can sing with
confidence, to find another young poet who rebels against the
fashionable pose that all is lost, all is despair. That he might
look to love as the redeemer will strike many as youthful. They
need be reminded that he is only restating the lesson of another
young man—the world's greatest teacher. That he finds anything, will gladden many who have not been able to subscribe
to the doctrine of futility. Love, however, is far from being the
only subject of his poetry. The wonder of the universe, the
nature of reality, and the nature of time alike hold his attention.
But above all is the quality of pity. He cannot hate. Evident in
the early poems and strongly present in *Vienna*, it is present in
the Judge and finds further expression in 'Two Armies' from
The Still Centre:

When the machines are stilled, a common suffering
Whitens the air with breath and makes both one
As though those enemies slept in each other's arms.

He has attempted with Auden and MacNeice the problem of detachment and even temporary self-exile in order to achieve a better perspective on a seemingly chaotic age in which great courage is necessary, if not for peace at least for an understanding of himself.

In his technique he follows Keats; in his idealism, Shelley; and in the elegiac tone, Arnold. His sensuousness frequently takes on an oriental quality, and his idealism holds up in the face of a world which strikes many as chaotic. He communicates his love of justice both directly and by ironic implication. Repeatedly he reveals his awareness of the century's ills, but like most thinking persons, he is unable to see the solution. Love and faith are necessary, but they are not enough. It is sufficient that Mr Spender has quickened our perception of the conditions about us. He has revealed aspects of his generation which would otherwise remain closed to us. His place in poetry is, of course, still undecided. His later work is not fulfilling the high expectations of many of his admirers. It is not that he has retrogressed, but that he has not advanced beyond the point of his early achievement. His mental sinews have not appreciably tightened.

LOUIS MacNEICE

W I T H the publication of *Autumn Journal*, described by its author, Mr Louis MacNeice, as 'something half-way between the lyric and the didactic poem,' it is possible to analyze with less tentativeness than would otherwise be possible the nature of his poetic contribution. The subject matter is political and differs in degree, from the collective subject matter of the later lyrics, in that it is an extension of those ideas. Easy criticism with its tendency to throw the work of Messrs Day Lewis, Auden and Spender into one basket and then to add that of Mr MacNeice for good measure errs through over-simplification. A certain time-spirit pervades their work, it is true, but each, conditioned by a different environment, is individualistic in his approach. Mr MacNeice is an Irishman and he frequently reveals traits that link him more closely with Yeats than with his contemporaries.

The earliest poems, interesting as metrical experiments and revelatory of the poet's imaginative power, carry little message, except, perhaps, for the semblance of a political note in the last stanza of 'Candle Poem.' The first such note appears in 'Spring Sunshine' when the beauty of the season, being the very devil in the poet, leads him to question the wisdom of man's devotion to the search for knowledge instead of surrendering himself to the sheer joy of living; just as in a later poem when spring tends to fool him into the belief of his ability for super-accomplishment, he must put the brakes on his enthusiasm. Over-introspectiveness in the attempt to find the solution to the unsolvable riddle of life is, he says, a vice of the age. Men from all classes realize that they are engulfed in spiritual desuetude, that the world is sick, and that life must be changed if they are to survive; but only the super-realists—the harlot 'inured forever to surprise' and the buffoon—will easily adjust themselves to the changes when they do occur.

In 1932 Mr MacNeice was not greatly interested in the constantly evolving political changes and confesses that he was somewhat of an anachronism. He felt then that he must build for himself a fortress 'against ideas and against the shuddering insidious shock of the theory vendors' ('Turf-Stacks'). He wanted as much as possible to give the illusion of permanency to the ephemeral things about him, and was willing to enjoy life's Vanity Fair, trusting on the fated day to escape with his dog. (In *Autumn Journal* he speaks of his dog as 'a symbol of the abandoned order.')

Being neither an alarmist nor an escapist, he has at no time been blind to reality. Happiness does not necessitate blindness to the frequent sordidness of life. He has seen man's self-preening tendency to take credit for advances in civilization for which he was in no way responsible. He has been alert to life, has sensed the plurality of the world in his awareness of the great variety of phenomena about him, and has realized that it is 'suddener than we fancy it.' A single phenomenon has opened his eyes to its wonder to the point of religious significance, and he deplores the average man's failure to appreciate it. God has set him up as a man but he is only painted wood with no real flesh and blood.

In 'Belfast' (1931), in 'Birmingham' (1933), and in his over-statement about Ireland—Section XVI of *Autumn Journal* (1939)—he reveals his awareness of the cruelty, hopelessness, and indifference of city life, particularly the slums, where no synthesis of life is made or attempted, where there is little thought, and where even the search for beauty is futile because pursued along the wrong paths—'harsh attempts at buyable beauty'—by shopgirls whose faces are 'diaphanous as green glass, empty as old almanacs.'

Although manifest from the beginning, the poet constantly affirms that he has no illusions about the everyday world being a 'desert in disguise'; but neither has he fear. There is no escape from the banality and purposelessness of life. He might

believe with Hardy that God is a logicless creator, but he
knows he can only find life by courageously outfacing the
'stare of stupidity and hate' on the faces of all classes and by

> making his minute assertion of human values:
> It is this we learn after so many failures,
> The building of castles in sand, of queens in snow,
> That we cannot make any corner in life or in life's beauty,
> That no river is a river which does not flow.
>
> *(Autumn Journal,* 11)

Man actually deserves much credit for the readiness with
which he adapts himself to 'domesticity, routine work, money-
making, or scholarship,' many of whom never suffer any disaster, 'never strike on the rock beneath the calm upholstering.'
Instead of wasting time regretting the inability to recapture
lost moments, we should be thankful for the happiness and
richness of our lives, for the 'sunlight on the garden.' Even the
starkest simplicity of life ('The Hebrides') has its beauty.

He realized in 1933, and even more vividly in 1939, that no
permanent escape from the 'week-day time' is possible; nor
does an association with age-old wisdom prevent restlessness.
And is it not paradoxical that when we think of life moving
steadily and inevitably like a glacier picking up persons ('dead
boulders') we look upon those persons caught up as the ones
who do not realize life to the fullest, but reserve that praise for
such as the scholar, the curator of the museum, or the gardener
who get out of the stream of traffic. Were we wise we should
emulate the may-fly who makes the most of his one day of life.

Mr MacNeice has maintained with increasing force, more
noticeable since his trip to Iceland in 1936 when he sought to
get a fresh perspective on life, to find

> Time for the soul to stretch and spit
> Before the world comes back on it,

that the person who too much ponders the meaning of life or

looks upon himself as superior to unreflective beings misses life. Intellect is valuable, but it can be harmful if by making one lose the sense of the great value of the little things it prevents an intimate contact with his fellow. In 'Ode,' a poem analogous to Yeats's 'A Prayer for My Daughter,' the poet prays that his son will not be a parrot crying with the mob, but a person who makes for himself a life rich in humanity and charity, one not too concerned with life's isolated minutiae, one who effects a synthesis of the world about him.

> For nothing is more proud than humbly to accept
> And without soaring or swerving win by ignoring
> The endlessly curving sea and so come to one's home
> And come to one's peace while the yellow waves are roaring.

Mr MacNeice also realizes that too many poets, being escapist, self-gratulating persons, suffocate the greater living beauty of the active life and try to justify their escapism. Escapism is blasphemy. The poet's 'privilege and panic' is 'to be mortal and with Here and Now' for his anvil he 'must strike while the iron is hot.' He must earn the right to pass the Gates of Death even if like those in Dunsany's 'The Glittering Gate' they open into nothingness. But he must not let himself be ensnared by the things that lie in ambush for his thoughts.

Obvious from the beginning, it has become steadily clearer that Mr MacNeice has revolted more strongly against 'The Waste Land'—'Ash Wednesday' tradition of poetry than have any of his contemporaries. In *Autumn Journal* he penetrates the snobbish surface erected as a protection from despair:

> None of our hearts are pure, we always have mixed
>   motives,
>   Are self deceivers, but the worst of all
> Deceits is to murmur 'Lord, I am not worthy'
>   And, lying easy, turn your face to the wall.
> But may I cure that habit, look up and outwards

And may my feet follow my wider glance
First no doubt to stumble then to walk with others
And in the end—with time and luck—to dance.

The apparently contradictory attitudes are, of course, expressions of one phenomenon—man's groping for a more mature spirituality.

Autumn Journal, wholly political, is the record of the poet's thoughts from August to December, 1938—the period of the Munich crisis and its aftermath. It denies none of the ideas of the later lyrics although written under the stress of immediate happenings rather than being the result of emotion recollected in tranquillity. The poet repeats with new emphasis his belief in the necessity for an improved social and economic order; criticizes the outmoded educational methods which prepare a boy for life of the old type, but not for life in a changing world; displays an increasing suspicion of abstract truth in favour of a truth based on our experiences and emotions in the present; and desires only to be

human, having a share
In a civilized, articulate and well-adjusted
Community where the mind is given its due
But the body is not distrusted
As it is, the so-called humane studies
May lead to cushy jobs
But leave the men who land them spiritually bankrupt
Intellectual snobs.

He realizes that those who by their habits hate politics must, if they would retain their private values, fight for a better political system. He is also aware that his statements on Ireland, Oxford, and Spain are over-statements; but one would not wish them different, particularly the caustically humorous one on Oxford.

No one, however conscious he may be of himself as a

member of society or of the political scene, devotes his whole time to it. Nor does Mr MacNeice do so in his poetry. The natural world absorbs much of his attention; and love, some, although the background remains essentially political. In 'Heated Minutes,' 'Passage Steamer,' and even more strongly in 'Leaving Barra,' one might question whether the political scene intensifies the love aspect, the love aspect the political scene, or if they are evenly balanced. 'For Services Rendered' unites politics and self-analysis with love. Only in 'Sonnet' is love the whole subject. The political theme in many lyrics, however, is little more than a focal point for an elaborate natural description of great force.

Mr MacNeice is not a poet content to hop on the band-wagon of some already established poet. Instances occur, in fact, to suggest that he is helping already-established poets to take a saner, less self-centred attitude towards life. With new force he brings home the necessity for a poet to be immediate. It is an accepted truism that his rank as a poet will rest on the way in which he has clothed the foregoing ideas, not on whether or not his ideas are acceptable. His greatest originality and vitality lie in the poetic clothing.

II

One of the most apparent ways in which Mr MacNeice differs from his contemporaries is in his use of prosodic form. He is a courageous if not always successful experimenter; and he has been less cautious in his later than he was in his early work. Although the early 'Glass Falling' bears a partial resemblance to a roundel, its interesting feature is the manner in which he plays with certain words. He repeats 'down' for example, with different meanings, literal as well as figurative. He is interested in assonance (clover—sober—cream-soda: 'The Individualist Speaks'), in half-rhymes (childhood-quiet-ude: 'Trains in the Distance'; shadow-meadow, placid-lucid, etc.: 'ForServices Rendered,') in interesting vowel combinations (the rooks bicker heckle bargain always: 'Spring Sunshine'); and in alliteration (. . . with the dull drumming of the sun suspended and dead . . .; and one feels the early going round and round the globe of the blackening mantle, a mad moth: 'Perseus'). He even pairs his half-rhymes (air-fur . . . thoroughfare-purr: 'Trapeze').

The stanzaic patterns vary in length from couplets to nine verses in a multiplicity of rhyme and rhythmic arrangement. His lack of rhyme, influenced no doubt by his close familiarity with classic forms is more frequent than that of rhyme, just as his use of regular stress is more frequent than verses of uniform syllabic length. In 'Passage Steamer,' the stanza is four-stressed, but the syllables vary from four to thirteen. The number of stresses varies from three ('Leaving Barra') to seven ('Museums'), the most frequent, however, being five. It is as usual to find several varieties of stress in one poem, as it is to find several types of rhyme in a poem that is chiefly non-rhyming. Nor should the reader be surprised to find each stanza in a poem with a different rhyme scheme ('August,' 'Mayfly,' 'Train to Dublin,' etc.). We might call the rhyme pattern of 'Leaving Barra' circular in design. The last word of each stanza is the last word of the first verse of the following stanza with the last word of the poem being the last word of the first verse of the first stanza. In his latest work, *Autumn Journal*, without dividing his verse into stanzas he uses a loose form of quatrain, rhyming a-b-c-b, made up of verses of various stresses. Traditional patterns occasionally occur. Our immediate concern with this wholesale array of patterns, however, is not with its extent but with the appropriateness of each as the poet uses it.

The first impression is one of greater passion in the more traditional forms; but immediately the question of associational overtone arises. Does greater passion exist or does it only seem to exist because of great familiarity with his medium?

Do they delight, as Mr MacNeice has himself expressed it,
'like a dead language which never shocks us by banal revela-
tions?' In many instances I believe the greater passion only
seems to exist. The pattern of 'Museums' is largely responsible
for the unmistakable quality of trenchant irony. The fears of
the child in the dark ('Intimations of Mortality') are heightened
by the movement of the stanza:

> After one perfunctory kiss
> His parents snore in conjugal bliss,
> The night watchman with crossed thumbs
> Grows an idol. The Kingdom comes . . .

In 'Birmingham' the couplets of varying length, built on a
variation of six, seven, or eight stresses catches the pulsation
of a vigorous city:

> Splayed outwards through the suburbs houses, houses for
>   rest
> Seducingly rigged by the builder, half timbered houses
>   with lips pressed
> So tightly and eyes staring at the traffic through bleary horns
> And only a six-inch grip of the racing earth in their con-
>   crete claws. . . .

In 'Hidden Ice,' however, would not the poet have achieved
a greater effectiveness of communication had he tightened the
texture. Where the patterns have jelled, as in 'Song' and 'The
Hated Minutes,' the passionate quality is heightened. Mr
MacNeice seems to have sensed this, too, because it is in the
later poems that we feel he has been most happy. 'June
Thunder,' 'Passage Steamer,' and 'The Hebrides' contain
technical devices that lift them above many of the earlier
lyrics. The short final verse in the stanzas of 'June Thunder,'
particularly the final 'Now if now only,' the repetition in the
second and fourth verse of each stanza of 'Passage Steamer,'
and the recurring refrain 'On those islands' of 'The Hebrides'

give a more ardent picture of the poet's heart, a more earnest sense of contrast, and a more poignant nostalgia, respectively, than would otherwise have been the case.

The movement of the verse in *Autumn Journal* is well adapted to the informal structure with its frequent over-statement and its lack of recalled emotion. The communication of an infectious care-free mood by means of the rollicking rhythm of a popular song is particularly noticeable in Section VIII, contrasting the easy life of 1931 with the present.

An interesting technical device is the use of internal rhyme in the following:

> Filleted sun streaks the purple *mist*,
> Everything is *kissed* and reticulated with sun—
> Scooped-up . . .;

and of internal half-rhyme in:

> But those who lack the peasant's conspirators,
> The tawny mountain, the unregarded buttress,
> Will feel the need of a *fortress* against ideas. . . .

or the use of 'oat-quote' in 'Eclogue By a Five-Barred Gate.'

Even better, however, are two examples from 'An April Manifesto':

> Man from his *vigil* in the wintry chapel
> Will card his skin with accurate *strigil*
>
> .   .   .   .   .
>
> Leave the *tedium* of audits and of finding correct
> For the gaiety of places where people collect
> For the paper rosettes of the *stadium and the plaudits*.

Instances of the foregoing are comparatively rare in *Autumn Journal*.

For sheer musical quality of a seductive kind we must turn to 'Evening Indoors' and 'The Creditor,' with the latter's

> . . . I lull myself
> In quiet in diet in riot in dreams
> In dopes in drams in drums in dreams
> Till God retire with the door shut.
> But
> Now I am left in the fire-blaze
> The peacefulness of the fire blaze
> Will not erase
> My debts to God. . .

Rhythm and image combine to form a particularly effective device in *Autumn Journal* in the use of surprise juxtaposition. 'Glory to God in the lowest,' 'if I had the cowardice of my convictions,' 'as I take the steep plunge to Henley or Hades,' are obvious examples. Better, however, is the following:

> The luxury life is only to be valued
>   By those who are short of money or pressed for time
> As the cinema gives the poor their Jacob's ladder
>   For Cinderellas to climb

with the idea of the fairy-tale Cinderella climbing the ladder on which Jacob in his dream saw the angels ascending and descending. Even more startling is the political connotation of the visit of the magi to the infant Christ:

> There was a star in the East, the magi in their turbans
>   Brought their luxury toys
> In homage to a child borne to capsize their values
>   And wreck their equipoise

The image of gaunt Conscience crying in the desert of contemporary civilization, close-linked with the 'herald angels' begging for copper coins startles the reader into keener attention:

> And Conscience still goes crying through the desert
>   With sackcloth round his loins:

A week to Christmas—hark the herald angels
  Beg for copper coins.

                          (80)

A surprise of a different kind is that found at the end of Section VIII. The pattern of the rhythm changes in the final verse and falls away, the reader following:

And stocks go up and wrecks
  Are salved and politicians' reputations
Go up like Jack-on-the-Beanstalk; only the Czechs
  Go down and without fighting.

III

It is probably already obvious to the reader that Mr Mac-Neice's distinction lies in the quality and wealth of his imagery, an imagery which only rarely gives the reader the sense of being a clever young man's straining after effect. In the earlier lyrics the images are apt to be too marked in their accent; but in *Autumn Journal* they are more effective for not being over-emphasized. They, as much as his direct statement of idea, reveal his alertness to the diverse phases of the world about him, natural and political. A reader unfamiliar with the world's events could readily tell from the frequency with which images pertaining to war occur that this was a war-conscious age. The drama and the variety show, music, the domestic arts, and social life likewise contribute their quota, and often in combination. Buttercups are 'gay gulps of laughter'; the falling blossoms are 'foam of may elder'; the lawn-mower spirts 'its little fountain of vivid green'; and the sun

     . . . quilts the valley and quick
  Winging shadows of white clouds pass
  Over the long hills like the fiddle's phrase.

Particularly effective is 'cross-stitch' in

> Bird-song and postman's whistle
> Cross-stitch the morning airs,

and the irrevocable quality of lives in

> But I cannot deny my past to which my self is wed,
> The woven figure cannot undo its thread.

The poet achieves a sustained *tour de force* in his description of a bizarre sunset in 'Trapeze'; just as in 'Snow' he effects a telling condensation when he speaks of the great bay window

> Spawning snow and pink roses against it
> Suddenly collateral and incompatible.

An image of snow in 'To a Communist' echoes a conceit of Milton's Nativity Ode; better is one in *Autumn Journal*:

> this is the first snow;
> And soon the specks are feathers blindly sidling
> Inconsequent as the fancies of young girls
> And the air has filled like a dance-hall,
> A waltz of white dresses and strings of pearls.

The sea has also entered deeply into the poet's consciousness. One can see the heavy sea exploding 'its drunken marble amid gull's gaiety.' The combination of the different concepts of explosion, drunkenness and marble into an accurate description of water is particularly happy.

Images from nature vivify his thoughts on apparently unrelated matters. Wit is the essence of the characterization of the scholar's activity as

> . . . the minnow twistings of the latinist who alone
> Nibbles and darts through the shallows of the lexicon.

Fish also suggest the effect of music in 'Sunday Morning'— 'the notes like little fishes vanish with a wink of tails'—just as the sport of fishing illumines a man's life—

Having bitten on life like a sharp apple
Or, playing it like a fish, been happy.

Time evokes a host of figures, a few of which are forced; all
lose when, lifted from their context, they are paraded as movie
starlets. A few remain incomprehensible. What does he mean,
for example, when he speaks of 'time punched with holes like
a steel sheet'? When, however, he speaks of our past as never
entirely recoverable in memory ('April Manifesto') the 'series
of dwindling mirrors' is an apt choice:

We never come full circle, never remember
Self behind self years without number.
A series of dwindling mirrors, but take a tangent line
And start again.

Effective, too, is his description of the petrol pumps standing in semi-circles 'like intransigent gangs of idols,' and his
castigation of wives as 'dream-puncturing wives.' It is obvious
that the poet has made his own observations and has not
blindly followed others.

IV

Instead of following others, he tends, even, to lead them.
The statement of his attitude towards life not only owes
nothing to a poet such as Mr Eliot, but is a vanguard for Mr
Eliot's stand in *The Family Reunion*. Wordsworth's well-known
definition of a poet has consciously or unconsciously served as
Mr MacNeice's model. In a world harassed by distractions
that make those of Wordsworth's days pale by comparison he
has accepted his responsibility. He is a man speaking to men,
he possesses a lively sensibility, he is contemporary, and he is
original enough in his attempts to broaden the horizons of
poetry that he will be misunderstood by many. As I have
already mentioned when writing of Messrs Day Lewis,

Auden, and Spender, it is still too early for a final pronouncement on this younger group of writers. Each remains an
individual. Apart from certain political convictions the only
characteristic that Mr MacNeice shares with them is originality. He is bold in his inventiveness and his work gives no
hint that he will be content in his future work with weak
variations on already announced themes.